ONE SUNDAY
IN DECEMBER

ONE SUNDAY
IN DECEMBER

The 1958 NFL Championship Game
and How It Changed Professional Football

LOU SAHADI

Forewords by Gino Marchetti and Sam Huff

THE LYONS PRESS
GUILFORD, CONNECTICUT
AN IMPRINT OF THE GLOBE PEQUOT PRESS

The Lyons Press is an imprint of The Globe Pequot Press.

Text design by Libby Kingsbury

Library of Congress Cataloging-in-Publication Data
Sahadi, Lou.
   One Sunday in December: the 1958 NFL championship game and how it
changed professional football/Lou Sahadi.
      p. cm.
   ISBN 978-1-59921-320-0
   1. National Football League Championship Game (26th: 1958: New York
City) 2. Baltimore Colts (Football team) 3. New York Giants (Football team)
4. Football—United States—History. I. Title.
   GV956.2.N38S34 2008
   796.332—dc22

                                          2008024506

Printed in the United States of America
10 9 8 7 6 5 4 3 2 1

CONTENTS

For Susan . . . and a Sunday in Paris, May 2007.

FOREWORD *by Gino Marchetti*

THE 1958 NFL CHAMPIONSHIP GAME was all about a third down in the final quarter with some two minutes left to play and the Giants ahead by 3 points. I knew that Frank Gifford was going to get the ball, and I felt that he would run right and cut to the left. I told everyone on the Colts line to hold their ground. I took two steps toward Giants tackle Jack Stroud to force Gifford to go wide. Gifford was determined to cut back, but he was too far outside, and I nailed him short of the first down by about a yard. Then, I thought, what are they going to do now with a precious yard to go to seal a 17–14 win? They decided to punt, which was the right thing to do, even though Giants fans were hollering to go for it.

Every time I walk, I remember that game. I broke my ankle on the Gifford tackle, and something didn't heal right, so I've got a bit of a problem with my ankle, my whole leg. Frank says he's sure he made the first down. Well, Frank doesn't know what he's talking about. From where I was lying, he didn't make it.

Frank was funny. He was hollering, "Get your damned butt off the ground, Gino." I guess he thought I was faking it to get an additional time-out. I said, "Frank, I can't get up. I can't." Big Daddy Lipscomb fell over my leg, that's how the ankle got broken. Most guys in football get hurt by their own players.

I wanted to see the end of the game. I told the Colts crew to put me down on the stretcher in the end zone. I did see Steve Myhra's field goal to tie it, and I saw the drive that John Unitas put together to get us there. Then, when it went into sudden death, they took me off. They were afraid that with one great play or something, the field would be crowded with spectators, and they wouldn't be able to get me out of there.

I was in a lot of pain. Still, I wanted to see the end, and they wouldn't let me. They took me down into the locker room, which was as quiet as could be, and I couldn't hear a thing. I didn't know what was happening, who was winning. I didn't know a thing until one of the players—Ray Brown, I think it was—came bursting into the room yelling, "We're the greatest!"

Imagine being in a game like that and not seeing the end of it.

I was with Baltimore when we used to get beat so bad that making a first down was a moral victory. In 1955, when we got Alan Ameche and Jack Patera and George Shaw and Ray Berry and George Preas—we had that fantastic draft, where I think we got eight guys who made the team big—it started turning around. And winning the championship, after being so bad a few years ago that we'd be down 45 to nothing at halftime . . . well, it was just a big thrill, something we worked so damned hard to get.

The Giants had beaten us during the season. It was a game when John was hurt and didn't even play. Shaw was the quarterback, and they won, like, 24–21. Then we got all the clippings from the *New York Times* and all the other papers where Frank and Charlie Conerly were saying, "We outgutted them"—you know, talking about what a great job they did—so that made us want to beat them even more.

In that championship game, I'd have to say that Weeb Ewbank gave probably the best pep talk he'd ever given, prior to the game. There are a lot of pep talks so awful that, you know, you laugh at them. But he went down everyone on the roster and had something for them. For instance, Artie Donovan. He said, "Dunny, the Cleveland Browns didn't want you, they traded you. And the New York Yanks cut you. Now you're here—show 'em how good you are." And he had a thing about Ameche and a thing about me. Everybody. I think that was the best pregame speech he ever gave. What a game.

FOREWORD *by Sam Huff*

WE WERE DOG TIRED AT the end of the fourth quarter when one of the officials shouted, "Overtime." I yelled back, "What overtime? We're tired. Let's call it a tie and split the money." I was all for that. I was only making $7,000 a year, and splitting some $4,000 of the championship money sounded good to me. I don't know how much football any of us had left. We had played an extra game the week before to reach the NFL championship with a playoff against the Cleveland Browns for the Eastern Conference title, and we were physically spent.

We had gone through the wringer to get this far, we were banged up after playing an extra game, and now we had to play one of the most potent offensive teams in the history of the game. The Colts were murdering everyone that year. John Unitas was throwing to people like Raymond Berry and Lenny Moore and could also give the ball to Alan Ameche, while the defense had guys like Gino Marchetti, Art Donovan, and Big Daddy Lipscomb. Before we'd go into a game against the Colts, Tom Landry always used to say, "The score is 7 to nothing, and we haven't even kicked off yet." We knew the Colts were going to score on us, and we knew we couldn't afford any mistakes.

We knew it, but we couldn't keep mistakes from happening. Frank Gifford fumbled twice in the first half, and we trailed at the half, 14–3. Early in the third quarter, the Colts really had our backs to the wall with a first and goal at the Giants 3. Back in the huddle, we were starting to get steamed up. We were acting like crazy men, and the feeling was there was no way we were going to let them get in and turn this thing into a rout. Ameche gained 2 yards to the 1, but Unitas tried to sneak it in on second down, and we stopped him. Ameche came to us on third down, and Rosey Brown and I tackled him short. On fourth down, Unitas got cute. He thought we'd be expecting Ameche up the middle; instead he threw him a pitchout to the right side. Cliff Livingston smelled it coming and stopped Ameche for a 4-yard loss, and the offense took over.

On the next series, we had third and 2 on our own 13 when Charlie Conerly crossed the Colts up by calling for a long pass after a fake pitch to Gifford. Kyle Rote was wide open over the middle and just kept running, though he was caught from behind at the 25 and had the ball stripped. Alex Webster was trailing the play. He scooped the ball up on the dead run and made it down to the 1. From there, Mel Triplett, our fullback, bulled in for the score, and we were back in the game, trailing 14–10. Early in the fourth quarter, Gifford atoned for his earlier fumbles by catching a 15-yard touchdown pass from Conerly, and Pat Summerall's extra point gave us a 17–14 lead. But with Unitas around, everyone in the stadium knew it was hardly the time to breathe easy.

We turned up the pressure again on defense, and Unitas couldn't move his team. Late in the period, Unitas had a second and 6 at our 27, but Andy Robustelli beat tackle Jim Parker and sacked Unitas for an 11-yard loss. Then it was Dick Modzelewski's turn. He came up through the middle and got Unitas again for a 9-yard loss. On fourth and 26, the Colts had to punt, and all we needed were a couple of first downs to wrap up our second NFL title in three years.

We got one of them on a 10-yard pass to Webster. But on third and 5 at our own 40, the game turned. Gifford took the ball from Conerly and was moving wide to the right up the field. He was tackled by Marchetti, and as they went down, Gene Lipscomb came over and fell on the pile. The impact was enough to break Marchetti's ankle, and he was on the field screaming and writhing in pain. In the confusion, the ball was spotted about

6 inches short of the first down. There's no doubt in my mind that Frank got that first down. But the referee picked up the ball and actually moved it back, and now Coach Jim Lee Howell had a tough decision to make. The crowd was going crazy; they wanted him to go for the first down, but Howell sent in the punting team, and I do believe it was the right decision. We had the lead, and we had Don Chandler, the best punter in the league, and we had the best defense in the game. There wasn't much time left, so you figure there was no way they could score a touchdown, and Steve Myhra, their kicker, wasn't very good; he'd only made four of his ten field goal attempts all year and was hardly known as a pressure kicker. Howell clearly made the right choice, no question in my mind about that.

Chandler's punt got the ball to the Colts 14-yard line, and we thought we were sitting pretty when Unitas fired two incomplete passes. But on third and 10, he found Moore open for an 11-yard gain, and the drive stayed alive.

At that point, we were playing a little looser, trying not to give them anything deep. Unitas took full advantage of that. On second and 10, he found Berry open over the middle with single coverage by Carl Karilivacz and hit him for a 25-yard gain to midfield. Next play, same combination, Unitas to Berry for 15 yards, Karilivacz trying futilely to defend. Unitas went to Berry one more time, for a 22-yard gain to the 13. Poor Carl; he blamed himself for years for that loss, but it wasn't his fault. Unitas had moved them 62 yards in the time it takes to blink, and Myhra surprised everyone in the stadium, and probably himself, too, when he kicked a 20-yard field goal to send the game into sudden death.

At that point, a lot of us knew we were in very deep trouble. We were exhausted from that last series, and Unitas and Berry were just on fire, and there didn't seem to be anything we could do about it. His linemen were blocking as if his very life depended on it. Our offense didn't help us on the first series after we won the coin toss. Conerly couldn't get anything going, and Chandler came on to punt.

The Colts took over at their own 20 and never gave up the ball again. Twice we had Unitas in third and long situations on the drive, and twice he found receivers open—first Ameche for 8 yards, then 21 yards to Berry for a first down at the Giants 43. The next play was the killer. Unitas called a trap and gave the ball to Ameche. He rumbled up the middle for 23 yards to our 20, and four plays later, Unitas crossed us up one last time by throwing a pass to his tight end Jim Mutscheller on second and goal from the 7 that carried to the 1. From there, Ameche got the ball and bulled over for the touchdown that gave the Colts the game and the title.

Why was it the greatest game ever played? Well, you had one of the most prolific offensive units in the history of the league playing against one of the most dominant defenses. There were Hall of Famers everywhere you looked on both sides of the line. It was the first time a championship had been decided by sudden death overtime, and there were millions watching on national television. It had everything—great offense, great defense, a lot of controversy. Hell, I even got in a fight with Colts coach Weeb Ewbank. I had tackled Berry on the sideline early in the game, a legitimate hit, but Weeb thought I was roughing up his man, so he took a poke at me when I got up. He didn't hurt me; he surprised me more than anything, and I kind of laughed at him. But it was just one of those things that happened in the heat of battle.

At the time, I don't think any of us realized the impact the game would have. I knew it cost me some money: the Colts' share was $4,674.44, and we got $3,083.27. We had let another opportunity for a championship slip away, and you don't get a lot of those chances in life.

I also knew that I had been involved in one of the toughest, most physically demanding games I'd ever played in. Was it the greatest game ever played? It sure felt like it. But when the 1958 game was over, it was gone forever, and I've always felt a little sad about that because it wasn't just any football game, it was a game for the ages.

PREFACE

ROB KIRKPATRICK DESCRIBED IT BEST: *persistence*. Rob, whom I only knew at first as a senior editor at Lyons Press, had used the word in my quest to have this book published.

I had written twenty others, but this one was special. As a young magazine editor in New York in 1958, I was spellbound by the most dramatic game ever played in the city and in the NFL, and I was compelled to write it as a once-in-a-lifetime occurrence. In the dead of winter, the entire city was on a week-long intoxication following the Giants' victory in a playoff game against the Cleveland Browns. The time had to be preserved in a book.

In June 2006, I had solicited the major houses in New York that had published many of my earlier books. The rejection letters solicited praise for a thirty-page proposal that included several partial sample chapters but no contract. I knew the material I had was good, much like my definitive biography of Johnny Unitas (*America's Quarterback*), which had also at first been turned down by the book houses. But I found a favorable one, and the Unitas book will be turned into a major motion picture in 2009.

I found a word in return for Rob: *insight*. The book came to life with an editor and an author through old-fashioned conversation, not by e-mails and faxes, which cannot deliver the soul of a book, and so many times are not even answered.

Rob, thanks for sharing the same vision I did and bringing *One Sunday in December* to a deserved place in bookstores.

I would also like to thank Peter Fierle, Matt Waechter, Jon Kendle, Saleem Choudry, Doug Murphy, Phyliss Hayes, Craig

Kelley, Ron Glass, Rebecca Leaming, Dusty Mormando, Herb Yale, Carol Jenkins, Greg Michie, Juan Delgado, Ben Levine, Tom McCarthy, Jan Cronan, John Burbidge, and especially Lynn McClary, a punctilious assistant every author should be fortunate to have.

Lou Sahadi
May 2008

INTRODUCTION

IT WASN'T SIMPLY JUST A championship game. It turned out to be more than that. Much more. It was history being made. The one quintessential championship game on December 28, 1958, in New York's Yankee Stadium between the Baltimore Colts and the New York Giants forever changed the landscape of the NFL. The high drama of the first sudden death game in the history of the league ushered professional football into the television era as a bona fide sport that was embraced by millions of new fans across the country. Decades later, every Colts and every Giants who played in this spectacular game with a Hollywood ending could look back and say, with complete honesty, "We played one for the ages . . . we played one for the league . . . we played one for the day that pro football grabbed an entire nation."

Sports Illustrated caused it to be called "The Greatest Football Game Ever Played" but didn't actually use the word *greatest*. Tex Maule, the magazine's pro football curator, wanted to use the word, but the magazine had a rule against it, and they settled on the word *best*. People all across America got the idea anyway. The game was heroically contested, a fierce confrontation between two self-anointed underdogs. The Giants weren't expected to be there, while the Colts were the have-nots of the league. But Johnny Unitas, a quarterback nobody wanted, had a Cinderella season.

◆

It was vastly different for pro football back then. *Sputnik* and *beatnik* were buzzwords. Detroit's automobile designers added rocket fins to the Cadillac. Elvis and Ike were in. So were Marlon Brando and Marilyn Monroe. Sugar Ray Robinson won the middleweight boxing championship for the fifth time, and a young golfer named Arnold Palmer won his first Masters Championship. Television was in, too. There were more black-and-white sets than ever before. If your family wasn't lucky enough to have one yet, you went to a friend's house to watch Dinah Shore, Ed Sullivan, *Playhouse 90,* or *You Bet Your Life.*

Pro football was not in. Oh, there was some provincial interest among the twelve franchises, and the sport had pockets of rabid fans, but nothing big. For most of the population, pro football was a nonexistent sport, something that took place when baseball was over. Instead, the college game was king. It was an era of thirty-five-men rosters, full-house backfields, two-bar face masks, and conventional-style place kickers. There were no domed stadiums, no artificial play surfaces, no white shoes, no players' union, no TV timeouts, and no *Monday Night Football.*

But all that changed on that dark afternoon in Yankee Stadium in an electrifying sudden death thriller that galvanized a nation. Years later, NFL Commissioner Pete Rozelle said that game changed the perception of professional football and brought more fans to the NFL than any other game.

"In years to come," wrote Gene Ward the next day in the *New York Daily News,* "when our children's children are listening to stories about football, they'll be told about the greatest game ever played—the one between the Giants and the Colts for the 1958 NFL championship. They'll be told of heroics the likes of which never had been seen."

Fifty years later, it has never been rivaled.

Time Capsule: 1958

It was a decade known as the Fabulous Fifties. As 1958 dawned, Hawaii was awaiting statehood. On January 31, the United States began its excursion into space when the Army orbited the first successful space satellite, *Explorer I,* from Cape Canaveral. Almost simultaneously, the campaign for nuclear disarmament was launched in February, ironically, a month before Nikita Khrushchev was elected to power in the Soviet Union in what was soon to begin an era in East–West relations known as the Cold War.

South Americans still looked upon the U.S. government as the Ugly American. In what was supposed to be a goodwill tour of the continent, Vice President Richard Nixon was greeted by anti-U.S. pamphlets in Uruguay, stoned in Peru, and spat upon in Venezuela. That same spring, the recession in the States reached major proportions, and by the summer, the unemployment rate peaked at 7.5 percent, the highest of the decade.

In June, events in North Africa and the Middle East began to boil. An insurrection in French-controlled Algeria returned Charles de Gaulle to power in France. By July, the U.S. presence in the Middle East was felt, as President Dwight Eisenhower dispatched troops to Lebanon to save the region's only democracy. It was just about that time the Baltimore Colts reported to training camp in Westminster, Maryland, with high hopes to win their first Western Conference championship. It was also reported in newspapers on July 10 that thirty-two-year-old Robert Earl Hughes, the world's heaviest human at 1,067 pounds, died in Bremen, Indiana.

It didn't get any better for Ike. On September 22, his closest adviser, Sherman Adams, resigned after it became known that he had accepted bribes. Also that month, Ike was greeted in Washington by some 10,000 black and white students in a "Youth March for Integrated Schools," which was, in reality, the first sign of a wave of student activism. By November, the Catholic Church had a new pope with the election by the College of Cardinals in Rome of Angelo Guiseppe Roncalli as John XXIII. By year's end, Fidel Castro had begun to make rumbles in Cuba, while the John Birch Society was formed in America.

The year's Nobel Prize for Literature went to Boris Pasternak for his work *Dr. Zhivago.* In the field of technology, the U.S. made history when the nuclear-powered submarine *Nautilus* passed beneath the North Pole, while New York theatergoers made a box office smash of Leonard Bernstein's *West Side Story.* Meanwhile, the rest of the country was dancing to the music of Bill Haley and His Comets as the hula-hoop craze reached its peak.

It was also a big year for Italian-American singers. Frank Sinatra was back on top following his Oscar-winning role in *From Here to Eternity* with such hits as "Three Coins in the Fountain" and "Love and Marriage" five years earlier. The other popular vocalists read like a Who's Who of Italian singers: Perry Como, Vic Damone, Tony Bennett, Dean Martin, Frankie Laine, Al Martino, Jerry Vale, and Mario Lanza. Only Johnnie Ray's "Cry" and Eddie Fisher's "Oh! My Papa" toned down the Italian hour, while Doris Day was number one among female singers with "Secret Love" and "Que Sera, Sera."

Elvis Presley's fans were saddened when he was inducted into the Army for two years as record sales took on a different look. Teenagers purchased 70 percent of all records pressed as the average age of pop music fans continued to drop. Among the top tunes were Domenico Modugno's "Volare" and Tommy

Edwards' "It's All in the Game." The Kingston Trio's "Tom Dooley" sold two million copies and marked the beginning of the folk craze.

In Hollywood, the Elizabeth Taylor–Eddie Fisher–Debbie Reynolds triangle made juicy headlines. In the world of sports, the New York Yankees reversed their 1957 defeat and won the World Series in a return meeting with the Milwaukee Braves, 4–3; Floyd Patterson retained his heavyweight title with a TKO of Roy Harris in the thirteenth round; and Althea Gibson once again won the USLTA women's tennis singles championship as Ashley Cooper won the men's title.

●

In professional football, the Baltimore Colts did manage to win their first ever NFL championship by defeating the New York Giants 23–17 in the first sudden death game ever played in league history behind a slightly bowlegged quarterback named Johnny Unitas. This seminal game captured the hearts of pro football fans around the country, ushering in the era of television and changing the Sunday afternoon habits of millions of Americans in the decades ahead.

In the fifty years since, the game left an immeasurable lasting impression. It deserves to be remembered as a piece of history. Its drama and excitement left a nation breathless beyond the playing field. Pro football and television were married that day, and the union flourished like no other sports entity in America. It was indeed the greatest game ever played . . . one Sunday in December.

TOOTS' SALOON

The Place to Be

The sports cognoscenti at Toots Shor's watering hole in mid-town Manhattan were a bit giddy on a cold December night in 1958. They had every right to be. It was three deep along the large mahogany bar, and there wasn't an empty table in the joint as the revelers toasted the New York Giants' incredible 10–0 victory over the Cleveland Browns hours earlier in an Eastern Conference playoff game in Yankee Stadium that sent the Giants into the NFL championship game. The very next Sunday they would face the Baltimore Colts in the venerable ball park in the Bronx where Babe Ruth once reigned. The crowd was in no hurry to leave. This night was all about celebration, and the Colts game could wait.

What the Giants had done, not only in the afternoon daylight but also a week before, had defied the odds that made the jubilation even louder. In the final regular season game in New York, they defeated these same Browns on a dramatic field goal in a snowstorm to extend the campaign another week and force a playoff to decide the Eastern championship. Pat Summerall, with a badly swollen knee, had missed a 48-yard field goal with four minutes remaining but miraculously got another chance two minutes from the end. In a surreal setting with hardly any other players recognizable and only the goal posts barely visible in the snow swirling around him, Summerall produced a kick for the ages. "After I missed the first kick, I wanted to go anywhere except back to the bench," disclosed Summerall in a happy Giants locker room. "I didn't see it go through. You couldn't see that far in the snow. But I knew. You could just tell."

No one was happier than Toots. Shor's was a sports crowd hangout, and Toots was as big a celebrity as the city's football and baseball heroes who frequented the place.

No one was closer to Joe DiMaggio than Toots. The restaurant was the Yankee star's home away from his hotel room. Joe was a loner and relished his privacy far removed from the fan adulation that made him the most popular sports figure in New York. The first time Toots ever met the Yankee Clipper, they forged an impregnable friendship. It was a peculiar union between a quiet, shy superstar and the big, boisterous Shor. They were indeed an odd couple but close nonetheless. After a bad game, DiMaggio would come by the restaurant and summon the doorman to get Toots, and the two would walk together up and down Fifth Avenue.

"No talking, not a word said about the game or my family or anything," revealed Shor. "He just felt like going for a walk. We hit it off the first time we met. Joe was just a great guy, very humble, very shy, but he was wonderful to my family."

Toots and DiMaggio were inseparable. Shor would rather see Joe hit than look at the *Mona Lisa*. He once knocked out a guy at Yankee Stadium for booing DiMaggio. A friend of both once saw Joe running down Sixth Avenue one afternoon and asked if anything was wrong.

"I just had lunch at 21, and I'm hurrying to Toots' to tell him before somebody else does," explained DiMaggio. "It wasn't my fault. Somebody in the Yankee front office invited me, and I couldn't say no."

"We're both stubborn," was how Toots explained the friendship. "We helped each other from the first time he came to New

York. I kind of brought him out of his shell. He was a very shy guy."

The Yankees were cognizant of the bond. And they were pleased. Ed Barrow mentioned to Yankee General Manager George Weiss that the relationship was perfect.

"Lucky we got Toots to be with Joe," admitted Barrow, the former GM.

Toots took it all in stride. That was his way. He never let anything bother him, and Joe was special.

"He didn't talk much, even to me, especially when there wasn't anybody else around," disclosed Shor. "One night he and Lefty Gomez and I were having dinner, and Lefty, as usual, was making everybody who came to the table laugh. Joe said to me, 'I wish I could be like Lefty, but I can't, and I know people who meet me go away saying to themselves that I'm a swell-headed Dago.'"

In reality, Toots' joint was summarily a men's club, where drinking was considered an art. It thrived on the camaraderie that only guys can gender, and Toots didn't look too kindly at wives. Whatever happened at Shor's stayed at Shor's, and that was what Toots was all about. It was known in the argot of the day as a place of booze and broads. He was a good friend of the Giants owner, Tim Mara, who was a good drinker himself and was as passionate about the Giants as his beloved Yankees. If you were one of Toots' guys, it was like being an elitist even in a gin joint. Toots' became the meeting spot not only for the locals but for every tourist who came to New York and stopped in. Shor's coarse, crass jibes were his trademark, which set him apart from others around him.

Three of his guys were Frank Gifford, Charlie Conerly, and Kyle Rote. One memorable occasion occurred when Gifford and Conerly, at Toots' invitation, took in Sinatra's show in Atlantic City. It resulted in an all-nighter. Was it ever. Toots was already flying high when the trio arrived in a limousine at the 500 Club. Sinatra's appearance attracted a large number of fans as well as the paparazzi outside the club, which was supposedly the property of the mob.

"Well, look at that," beamed Toots. "They're all waiting for us."

"Who's that?" shouted an onlooker.

"It's Tootsie," exclaimed Shor. "The world's prettiest Jew."

At the ringside table, Toots became a bit noisy. He kept yelling "Sinats," and Sinatra was getting annoyed. Someone, well dressed in a suit and tie, came over and put a lock on both of Toots' wrists. "That's enough," he growled. After Sinatra's performance, Gifford asked the maître d' who the guy was who shut up Toots.

"Fischetti," he remarked. "Big man from Miami. He and Sinatra are like brothers. Your friend is lucky he ain't dead."

All three of them were wasted, yet somehow Toots got them on a plane to Vermont the next morning for the opening of training camp. The bleary-eyed stars, blinded by the sun, were in search of a taxi when Giants Vice President Wellington Mara approached them carrying a newspaper with a photo of the two. "Need a ride?" he asked sarcastically and tossed the paper at them.

How Toots, with the face like an Irish potato and eyes that looked half closed for the most part, ever achieved royalty was something else again. He was born poor in South Philadelphia, a chubby youngster in a predominantly Irish-Catholic neighborhood.

At first, he wasn't accepted with open arms. Toots reached out, wanting to make friends, but he only encountered rejection to the degree of incurring fights. Yet Toots managed to outwit his tormentors, realizing his odds against three or four were not good. He concurred that by running through any Catholic church in his escape route, he could gain some valuable ground to safety.

"These bums would have to genuflect when they reached the altar," recalled Toots. "I didn't have to break stride." One such time he safely made it home from his run, breathless and teary eyed. His mother looked at him, puzzled. "They called me a Jew," he shouted. "Well, what did you say?" asked his mother. "I told them I couldn't help it." On another occasion when he didn't shake his pursuers, he came home with a swollen lip. His mother stared at him, wanting an explanation. "A boy hit me," he exclaimed. "Go out and hit the boy who hit you," ordered his mother without offering any sympathy.

But as Toots grew big and strong entering high school, the intimidation ceased. He was now one of the guys, and his popularity extended to the pool halls. He was a proficient shooter and began cutting classes to hustle some money. Toots, the pool shark, was how he was looked upon. It came to a halt when his parents were given a stern warning from school officials that he would be expelled.

By 1930 Toots was ready for New York, arriving there by bus. His first meal, he remembered, was in Bickford's, a cafeteria. That was the last time he carried a tray. He wanted the better life and embarked on his quest as a bouncer at a private club, one of the many around Manhattan. In four years, young Toots was a manager at one of them at $75 a week and a percentage of the take. It was the beginning of the good life made easier by Toots' gambling, which he was very good at. Yet, when 1939 dawned, Toots was married and broke, not a winning combination by any means. However, by September, Toots, backed by a couple of friends, opened his own place at 51 West Fifty-first Street, next to the posh 21 Club.

The night he opened the eponymous Toots Shor's, he had already had tradition, which translated into instant success. He called his large mahogany bar his "roulette wheel." He grossed $2 million in the bar he referred to as his "store," and there was never a dull night from that time on. By then, Jackie Gleason had fallen on hard times and asked Toots for a stake. A benevolent Shor accommodated him. One evening, Toots had asked Gleason not to tip so generously with his money.

"What," countered Jackie, "and have your waiters call you a cheap bastard?"

Toots had the greatest floor show in New York, and it didn't even cost him a dime. Toots and Gleason were an act in themselves, and they were inseparable. They drank together, ate together, went to the track and ball games together, and played golf together, or in Toots' case, played at it. One day, Shor was a horror, finishing eighteen holes with a 211.

"What should I give the caddy?" whispered Toots. "Your clubs," shot back Gleason.

Before Jackie hit it big with *The Jackie Gleason Show,* he was broke. Toots carried him and lent him money, never asking when he would pay it back. Their bond was that strong. "At one time he was into me for over $10,000," admitted Shor. "I gotta hand it to him, though. When he got into the big money, he came by and handed me the cash, saying, 'Here's what I'm sure I owe you.'"

They were always playing pranks on each other, with Gleason, of course, the instigator. One night, Jackie challenged Toots to a race around the block, with a wager being double or nothing on the bill. Toots agreed. But Gleason had one stipulation: that they would run in opposite directions. When Jackie was out of Toots' sight, he hailed a cab. A half block from Toots' place, Gleason got out of the cab and handed the driver $5. When a puffing Toots arrived at his saloon, Gleason was already there at the bar.

Toots' friends were dear to him, and he never ignored them, no matter what celebrity was in the joint. One night he was talking with Sir Alexander Fleming, who won the Nobel Prize for the discovery of penicillin, when New York Giants outfielder Mel Ott walked in. Toots didn't waste a second. "Excuse me, Sir Fleming," he apologized, "but I gotta leave you. Somebody important just came in."

That was only one part of the equation. Tonight was one of celebration. Shor's Giants and the Colts would go at each other the very next Sunday, and the Babe would be looking over his kingdom, hopefully this time without the snow. Once again, the Giants had been projected as underdogs against a Cleveland team that was balanced on both sides of the ball, with the imposing figure of fullback Jim Brown, a 235-pound power runner with sprinter's speed who averaged over 5 yards a run, offering the biggest challenge. He was by far the best runner in the league, one who could completely take over a game. In the nine years he would play, he led the NFL in rushing eight times, which nobody had ever done before or would again. He was that good.

The Giants were sculptured as a defensive unit. Led by middle linebacker Sam Huff, the defense positioned Giants victories all through the 1958 season.

Huff was the team's hallmark, and the cry of "Defense!" resonated throughout storied Yankee Stadium ever since the 1956 season, when the Giants first moved across the river to the Bronx, where they won the NFL championship by caging the Chicago Bears, limiting them to a single touchdown in a

47-7 rout. Huff's individual battles with Brown were classic, the stuff that documentaries were made of. On this Sunday, no one could have imagined what eventually occurred. With Huff dogging the brilliant running back every step of the way, the Giants restricted Brown to a miniscule 8 yards in a Rembrandt-painted shutout.

That was what all the jubilation was about on December 21, and, like the Colts, Christmas could wait. The Giants were Toots Shor's team, and the city's colorful innkeeper—a character who could have been created by famous New York writer Damon Runyon—took care of every one of them that came by. Toots affectionately referred to regulars like Charlie Conerly, Frank Gifford, and Kyle Rote as "My Boys." They spent many a late hour with Toots, and he treated them royally, the way he did with Joe DiMaggio and Mickey Mantle, though not necessarily together, in the summertime. "He knew all the mob guys," pointed out Gifford. "He liked them all, and why not? They gave him the opportunity to be Toots Shor."

Toots had his favorites from all walks of life, and if you were one of them, there was no tab. And Toots could drink with the best of them, from the city's politicians to John Wayne and Frank Sinatra and any other celebrity who wandered into his joint. He was a two-fisted Hennessy drinker and was always the last guy standing.

Toots lived the good life whether he was joking with his close pal Jackie Gleason; gassing with Walter Winchell, Damon Runyon, Walter Cronkite, Mike Wallace, Dwight Eisenhower, or J. Edgar Hoover; or rubbing elbows with some of the wise guys—Frank Costello and Jimmy Hoffa, in particular. He was always finely dressed, with a shirt and a tie and a large pinky ring.

Toots was an imposing figure, big and boisterous with a rotund face that could light up a room. His signature greeting was "Crumb bum." It was a show of endearment to those who were close to him. Gifford especially was that guy, with Conerly and Rote close behind. Gleason was very special. He would be a constant companion with Shor at Yankee games in the warmth of the summer and the Giants games in the chill of autumn.

Toots fancied himself as an old-fashioned saloonkeeper. That's how he wanted to be known, because in the old days, that's what owners were known as, and it was common for them to drink in their own joints. On some days, he would put away two bottles of brandy. Sinatra was never that good. Gleason was the only one who could keep up with him, all the while volleying barbs at each other. Good-natured fun. Jackie was in Toots' saloon practically every night of the week, which was just around the corner from CBS and *The Jackie Gleason Show*. One night the kidding began. "Beast," exclaimed Toots, "what are you doing in my joint?"

"The food here is the worst in America," answered Gleason. "Just look at this steak. This ain't food. This is garbage."

"You sure suck it up."

"Clamhead."

"Crumb bum."

But Gleason wasn't finished. "Clamhead, even the hamburger you buy is already rotten," he said. "I'll bet you $500 that if you took a pound of hamburger out of your refrigerator, it would turn green in a half hour."

Gleason knew that Toots never spent much time in the kitchen and knew nothing about hamburger meat, which loses its color when left out. He was too occupied drinking and mixing with the customers, the ones he preferred. Toots turned and called out to his maître d': "Get me a pound of hamburger."

Gleason and Toots stared at the raw meat as if they were look-ing at the Hope Diamond. At the appointed half hour, the ham-burger took on a brownish hue, much to Shor's amazement.

"I'm going to kick my chef's ass," vowed Toots, as Gleason gave his best $500 smile.

The Reverend Benedict Dudley, the Giants' team chaplain who appeared on the sidelines at every game, also appeared regularly at Shor's. He was known as Father Ben to the players. Coinci-dentally, he was from the same Philadelphia neighborhood as Toots, and that was enough of a bond to qualify him as a mem-ber of Toots' inner circle.

Although they were quite the opposites, a reserved member of the clergy with a foul-mouthed innkeeper, Toots respected Father Ben enough to set him up for the night with a straight-up manhattan. Of course, one would lead to another after a meal. Father Ben never got caught up in all the bar talk as he quietly sipped his manhattans. He went practically unnoticed until Toots would blurt out one of his four-letter expletives.

"Oh, excuse me, Father, excuse me," apologized Toots, who then continued whatever story he had started.

"A bum who ain't drunk by midnight ain't trying," claimed Toots.

Even though the food was mediocre, Shor's was an action spot, a magnet for tourists as well as the established regulars, along with the city's businessmen and their two-martini lunches. It wasn't unusual for diners to wait in line for a table or even a spot at the bar to catch a glimpse of a celebrity or sports star. If none appeared, they would at least leave with Toots' autograph on a menu. He never used any bad language with the visitors, but he could be testy with some of his remarks.

The cantankerous Shor was a master of the jibes, and he nonchalantly would direct them at any celebratory figure, especially if he wasn't part of Toots' inner circle of friends. One evening Charlie Chaplin was on line waiting to be seated. When the movie icon complained to Shor, he brusquely told Chaplin to entertain the others who were waiting, too. Another time, MGM chief Louis B. Mayer grumbled that he waited twenty minutes for a table.

"I trust the food will be worth all that waiting," snapped Mayer.

"It'll be better than some of your crummy pictures I stood in line for," retaliated Shor.

One evening a couple from Nebraska approached Shor and complained that they weren't satisfied with their meal. "We have better steaks in Omaha," they remarked. Toots wasn't fazed. "So what? When you're through eating your steak, you're still in Omaha."

Toots even got complaints by mail. A couple from the Midwest took the time to send him one, which, of course, never bothered the unflappable Toots:

My wife and I dined at your restaurant one night during a recent trip to New York. We found the food excellent, the drinks very nice, and the atmosphere and service fine. But if you expect to make a success in your business, you'd better get rid of that fat slob of a headwaiter who spent most of his time insulting patrons.

Toots was loved, and he remained being Toots even if his cantankerous ways might have offended someone along the way.
On his fiftieth birthday, his contemporaries gathered around
him and showed him love. The big guy was touched.

"We all gathered here to weep great, big slobbering tears for
a fat, drunken saloonkeeper," chided Red Smith of the *Herald
Tribune.*

Journalist Quentin Reynolds was more eloquent. "Not often
in the story of mankind does a man arrive on earth who is both
steel and velvet, who is as hard as a rock and soft as a drifting
frog," recited Reynolds, quoting Carl Sandburg.

It was a celebration that boasted the very best of a men's
club, and several more guests roasted Toots. But Toots would
have the final say.

"There is nothing which is contrived by man as that is pro-
duced at a good tavern or inn which is named a saloon, and
I know you fellows will agree with me," began Toots. "On Joe
DiMaggio Day at Yankee Stadium, Joe said, 'I'm lucky to be a
Yankee.' When Leo Durocher quit the Polo Grounds, he said,
'I'm lucky to be a Giants.'

"Sitting here looking at all you people, all I can say is I'm
lucky to be a saloonkeeper. I use and like the word *saloon.*"

&

Toots was always fast and good with the quips, and his joint
was a gold mine, yet it wasn't always this good for the Giants.
They had struggled during their many winters in the antiquated
Polo Grounds, which was eternally cold and damp, with a playing field that absorbed water from the adjacent East River. It
was an outdated wooden structure that had been around since
Ulysses S. Grant was president, that had seen better days with
John McGraw's baseball Giants and in modern times the 1951
and the 1954 championship teams of Willie Mays. As late as

1948, the football Giants were a debt-ridden team, one in which a local bank held heavy financial notes that weren't reconciled until the early 1960s. No one in Toots' that night knew that about their Eastern Conference champions, and with all the jubilation, nobody would have really cared. The revelers had an early Christmas, and three days later the Giants would take on the Colts for the NFL championship. How good was that?

There was no place like Shor's, and there was no one like Toots. Tonight was special. His Giants had won, and he was waiting for his boys, Gifford, Conerly, Rote, and whoever else came out of the winning dressing room to celebrate. It had all the components for an all-nighter.

Not even the city's crippling newspaper strike could expunge their merriment. No one could take this night away from them, and they deserved every moment of it. The year before they were betrayed and suffered with a yearlong exodus of the Brooklyn Dodgers and New York Giants to California, leaving baseball in New York solely to the Yankees.

In what was now a short year later, they had a team of their own, a contending one to cheer for on one more Sunday in December, which is when champions play.

Ohio Roots

There wasn't anything like Toots' place or anybody like Toots when the National Football League tried to become a part of America's sports landscape that Norman Rockwell began to indelibly illustrate. The nation passionately embraced baseball and college football and didn't have room for anything else. By 1920, the dawning of the golden age of sports helped the country recover from the horror of the Great War that had ended two years earlier. The decade was launched with Knute Rockne, Red Grange, and Ernie Nevers in football; Walter Johnson, Ty Cobb, Babe Ruth, and Lou Gehrig in baseball; Jack Dempsey and Gene Tunney in boxing; and Bobby Jones in golf. Americans had new heroes to cheer for, with the bitter memories of the war now behind them.

The selling of Ruth by the Boston Red Sox to the New York Yankees for $125,000, the largest sum ever paid for a player, shocked the sports world. As a pitcher with the Red Sox, Ruth, who hit twenty-nine home runs in 1919, asked for and received a $10,000 raise, to $20,000. The year also ushered in the beginning of Prohibition, but, even worse, the Black Sox scandal in September rocked baseball with the indictment of eight Chicago White Sox players, who were charged with conspiring with gamblers to fix the 1919 World Series.

Big Bill Tilden brought America pride by becoming the first American to win the Wimbledon tennis championship, while the nation's sweethearts, movie stars Douglas Fairbanks and

Mary Pickford, were married in Los Angeles, making June a month to remember. The horse racing set bid farewell to Man O'War, who retired after only one loss in twenty-one outings. His purse money amounted to a quarter of a million dollars, almost double the earnings of the other thoroughbreds.

●

Professional football was in flux, which was specifically generated by three major problems: players who were jumping from one team to another, dramatically rising player salaries, and the use of players still in college. Jim Thorpe, with the Canton Bulldogs, was the scattered league's highest paid player, at $250 a game. He was worth considerably more than the Green Bay team that entered the league a year earlier for $500. Attempting to rectify the burgeoning problems, an organizational meeting took place on August 20 in, of all places, an automobile showroom in Canton. Three teams, the Akron Pros, Cleveland Indians, and Dayton Triangles, joined the host Bulldogs, which resulted in the formation of the American Professional Football Conference with a distinct Ohio flavor. The meeting was considered the advent of the modern NFL.

A month later, another meeting took place in Canton. The four Ohio teams met with representatives from three other states: the Muncie Flyers and Hammond Pros from Indiana, the Rock Island Independents, Decatur Staleys (named for the A. E. Staley Company and its owner), and Racine Cardinals from Illinois; and the Rochester Jeffersons from New York. They dropped the word *Conference* and substituted *Association* and, at the same time, named Thorpe president, with the idea that his popularity would produce more recognition for the embryonic association. They also voted to assess a membership fee of $100, which, sadly enough, none of the teams honored. In reality, it was simply a paper league with little or no substance.

On September 26 the first APFA game took place in Rock Island, as an estimated crowd of 800 watched the Independents defeat the St. Paul Ideals 48–0. The Minnesota team, along with the Buffalo All-Americans, Chicago Tigers, Detroit Heralds, and Columbus Panhandles, brought the league's membership to fourteen teams. However, at season's end, Detroit and Chicago dropped out, and with no title game scheduled, Akron was looked upon as the champion by being the only unbeaten team. The Bulldogs also took part in the first player deal ever made by sending tackle Bob Nash to Buffalo for $300.

On March 21, 1921, Warren Harding was sworn in as the nation's twenty-ninth president and promised no foreign entanglements. America began to feel good about itself. On a hot July day, 100,000 fans turned out on Boyle's thirty acres in New Jersey and witnessed Jack Dempsey's fourth-round knockout of France's Georges Carpentier. Rudolph Valentino made women swoon starring in the movie *The Sheik*. Babe Ruth thrilled baseball fans by hitting fifty-nine home runs that year, but the Yankees lost the World Series to the New York Giants.

Lillian Gish's romance with "Diamond Jim" Brady became legendary in 1922 and was talked about more than the APFA. The first edition of *Reader's Digest* was published, while King Tut's tomb was discovered by two British Egyptologists. There were rumblings on the other side of the globe. British authorities sentenced Mohandas Gandhi to six years in prison for sedition in the spring, while in the fall, Benito Mussolini's Fascists marched on Rome.

Two months later, on January 27, 1923, the Nazi Party held its first congress in Munich under the leadership of Adolf Hitler's National Socialist Party, while in Berlin, one loaf of bread was worth 140 billion marks as Germany was still suffering from its defeat in World War I. Former president Harding died in San Francisco, while the great tragedienne Sarah Bernhardt succumbed at age seventy-eight in Paris.

The following year, former president Wilson died in his sleep a month after the first Winter Olympic Games debuted in Chamonix, France. Gene Tunney took care of the Frenchman Georges Carpentier with a fifteenth-round KO. Two months later, Hitler was sentenced to five years in prison but was released on December 20. Three famous births occurred in September—Truman Capote, Lauren Bacall, and Marcello Mastroianni—while ten-year-old actor Jackie Coogan met the pope in Rome and remarked: "Best place in the world for shooting pictures after Hollywood!"

Over those four years, the APFA continued to struggle but managed to survive. Surprisingly, membership had risen to twenty-two teams but by 1924 had fallen to eighteen. Still, some significant occurrences evolved during the period. In 1921 Thorpe left Canton and joined the Cleveland Indians; Staley turned over his team to player-coach George Halas, who relocated the franchise to Chicago (Staley paid Halas $5,000 to maintain the name Staleys for one year, which Halas gladly accepted); and the Akron Pros' Fritz Pollard became the first black coach in the league. That year, the Staleys, with a 9–1–1 record, and Buffalo, with an 9–1–2 mark, each laid claim to the APFA championship. There still wasn't a title game to decide it, and league president Joe Carr named the Staleys as champions.

"Right at the beginning, I put down a set of rules for the players," said Halas. "Rules about things the pro teams never thought about in those days: curfews, meetings, and practices. I asked myself what must our players do in order to be complete football players on Sunday. One thing I insisted on was daily practice, which was something the other teams did not have."

The National Football League banner made its first appearance in 1922 at a meeting on June 24, and at the same conclave the Bears became Chicago's new nickname. Green Bay, which was on life support, was resuscitated by local merchants with a $2,500 loan as a nonprofit corporation, with Curly Lambeau as head coach and manager. For two consecutive years, Canton emerged as league champions, the result of unbeaten seasons of 10-0-2 and 11-0-1. Despite their success, fan support was anemic, and the franchise was deactivated. The Bulldogs' best players were added to nearby Cleveland, and they contributed to produce a 7-1-1 record and the league championship.

⬤

While Walter Chrysler formed the Chrysler Corporation in Detroit in 1925 and the Charleston was the newest dance craze, the devilish Hitler published his book, *Mein Kampf,* or *My Struggle*. The years were paramount for the tireless owners of the NFL, as it was still second in popularity to the college game. It took a college superstar to provide the league with impetus and suddenly a brighter future for its newest five teams: the New York Giants, Providence Steam Roller, Detroit Panthers, a new Canton Bulldog team, and the Pottsville Maroons, the most successful independent team.

Almost immediately after the University of Illinois finished its season in November, All-American halfback Harold "Red" Grange signed a contract to play for the Bears. "On the field, he is the equal of three men and a horse," was the way heralded columnist Damon Runyon described him. On Thanksgiving Day, the largest crowd in pro football history, 36,000 in number, pushed their way into Wrigley Field and saw Grange and the Bears play a scoreless tie with the Cardinals, the city's other team.

A week later, Grange and the Bears went on a barnstorming tour, playing a phenomenal eight games in twelve days that included the major cities of New York, Philadelphia, Detroit, Pittsburgh, Chicago, Boston, Washington, and St. Louis. The game against the Giants attracted a staggering 73,000 fans. The Bears continued to play nine more games in the South and West. When 75,000 fans made their way into the Los Angeles Coliseum, the league headed into a new era, with Grange as the magnet needed to secure popularity. His biggest highlight was not on the field but in meeting Babe Ruth in New York. "Kid, I'll give you a little bit of advice," disclosed Ruth. "Don't believe anything they write about you, good or bad. And, further, get the dough while the getting is good, but don't break your heart trying to get it."

Grange's manager, C. C. Pyle, agreed with the Babe's advice. He informed the Bears that Grange would not play in the 1926 season unless he received a five-figure contract and one-third ownership of the Bears. Halas immediately refused. However, the ambitious Pyle wasn't finished. He secured a lease for Yankee Stadium and petitioned the league for a franchise but once again received a refusal. Undeterred, he formed the American Football League with Grange as the flag bearer. Unfortunately, the eight-member league lasted only one season.

America had a new hero that summer when Bobby Jones won the British Open and still another that fall when Gene Tunney took the heavyweight title away from Jack Dempsey before 130,000 fans in Philadelphia, while Greta Garbo's beauty captivated Hollywood.

The NFL found another star attraction in Stanford All-American halfback Ernie Nevers to rival Grange and his upstart league. Playing for Duluth, Nevers and the fifteen-member Eskimos played twenty-nine exhibition and league games, twenty-eight of which were on the road. Remarkably, Nevers performed in all but twenty-nine minutes of them as Duluth was dubbed, and rightfully so, the "Iron Men of the North." Nevers and the Eskimos dominated the headlines; little attention was given to the fact that the Frankford Yellow Jackets edged the Bears, without Grange, 7–6, to move ahead of them in the standings and lay claim to the championship.

●

By 1927 America had become the land of the automobile, with Americans owning 39 percent of the world's total. Individually, four Americans stood alone. In April Johnny Weissmuller set two world records in swimming, Charles Lindbergh became the first to fly the Atlantic alone nonstop from New York to Paris in thirty-three hours and was cheered by 100,000 Parisians in May, and Babe Ruth hit his sixtieth home run of the season in Yankee Stadium in September. Tunney retained his title in the famous "long count" fight with Jack Dempsey.

That same year produced the NFL's most defining moment during a special meeting on April 23. Carr decided to ensure the NFL's future by eliminating its financially weaker cities. The once twenty-two-member circuit was drastically reduced to twelve, and the balance of power represented by the Midwest, where it all began, was shifted to the larger cities of the East. Grange appeared with the Yankees but missed a large part of the season with a knee injury as the cross-town rival Giants became the league champions. "After that, I was just another halfback," lamented Grange.

It was time for a female heroine in America. On June 18, 1928, Amelia Earhart became just that in becoming the first woman to fly across the Atlantic, landing in South Wales in twenty-two hours. But change was also taking place. On November 23 the highest trading in Wall Street history shut down the stock market after a record number of shares (6,954,020) were sold. Change also permeated the NFL, as both Grange and Nevers retired. It was all about the money. They realized their star status sold tickets, and they wanted to be compensated accordingly. It left a rippling effect on the NFL, which was left with only ten teams.

Grange and Nevers made their economic point and returned for the 1929 season. Playing for the Cardinals, Nevers made a prodigious impact, scoring six touchdowns and 4 extra points in a November 28 game against Grange and the Bears, 40-6. The 40 points Nevers produced set a record that has withstood time and remains the oldest one in league history. Three weeks earlier, the Cardinals had been the first to take part in a night game at Providence. Yet it had been the beginning of a devastating time in America. On October 24, the stock market crashed, with nearly thirteen million stocks changing hands in what was called Black Thursday. The Great Depression was about to cripple the economy and spread hardship for families all across the country.

The Depression didn't affect Babe Ruth's earning power. He signed a contract for the unheard of amount of $160,000, which was $80,000 more than President Herbert Hoover's salary. When asked about it, the colorful Babe quipped, "I had a better year than he did." Somehow, William Dwyer and John Depler found enough money in 1930 to purchase the Dayton Triangles, the last of the league's original franchises, moved them to Brooklyn, and renamed them the Dodgers. The same year the Portsmouth Spartans joined the league as Halas retired as a player and turned over his coaching duties to Ralph Jones, who gave the T formation a completely new look by splitting both ends and setting a halfback in motion. Jones also had a new weapon in an All-American fullback who also played tackle, Bronko Nagurski, who would become the NFL's next big star.

"When you hit him," warned Grange, "it was like getting an electric shock. If you hit him above the ankles, you were likely to get yourself killed."

Still, the league remained unsettled. Halfway through the 1931 campaign, the Frankford franchise closed its doors. The Packers began developing their legacy under Lambeau by winning the championship for an unprecedented third consecutive season. While Packers fans took pride, the rest of the nation showed signs of progress. Two major architectural marvels were unveiled that year: the George Washington Bridge, spanning 3,500 feet above the Hudson River and linking New York and New Jersey, and New York's Empire State Building, the tallest in the world at 1,453 feet and 102 stories. Major Jimmy Doolittle provided a boost to domestic air travel by making three fuel stops on his flight from California to New Jersey in eleven hours, sixteen minutes.

When the 1932 season dawned, the league awakened with only eight teams, the smallest in its maturing history, which certainly didn't bode well for its future. But that was miniscule compared to what was transpiring around the country. The New York banks agreed to lend the city $350 million, while President Hoover set aside $2 billion to pump up industry and create jobs for the eleven million Americans out of work. The taxing Depression was reason alone for Franklin Delano Roosevelt to win the presidency in a landslide. Somehow, 95,000 had a few bucks to witness the closing of the Olympics in Los Angeles, which probably was more than attended all of the NFL games. When the season ended, the Bears and the Spartans finished in a first-place deadlock. The league scheduled a playoff for Chicago on December 18, which was fine until Old Man Winter showed up early. Fierce snow and an arctic cold forced the game to be played indoors in Chicago Stadium. The Bears beat the Spartans 9–0, the only touchdown coming on a controversial forward pass from Nagurski to Grange.

At his inauguration on March 4, 1933, Roosevelt uttered his famous remark to a beleaguered nation, "The only thing we have to fear is fear itself," while casting a wary eye on Hitler, who had become chancellor of Germany. With doubt about the NFL's existence hovering until spring, the eight teams not only survived but found three more members as well. Art Rooney and the Steelers represented Pittsburgh, Bert Bell did the same with the Philadelphia Eagles, while Lud Wray introduced the Cincinnati Reds, giving the league a completely new look. Halas and George Preston Marshall fostered a proposal dividing the NFL into two divisions. Halas became sole owner of the Bears, while Marshall assumed control of the debt-ridden Braves (later named Redskins) in Boston. Splitting the NFL in two allowed the league for the first time to schedule a championship game before the season began. When it concluded on December 17, the Western Division Bears defeated the Eastern Division Giants, in Chicago, 23–21, as Halas made a triumphant return to the sidelines.

America's economy was still sagging in 1934 as FDR devalued the dollar to sixty cents. It wasn't a good year for gangsters either, as four of the notorious ones, Bonnie Parker and Clyde Barrow, John Dillinger, and Baby Face Nelson, were gunned down by federal agents, while two international ones, Hitler and Mussolini, met for the first time in Venice. That August Halas and his Bears provided some much needed prestige to the league. Before 79,432 fans in Chicago, the Bears and the College All-Stars played to a scoreless tie at Soldier Field. When the regular season opened weeks later, the Spartans found themselves in Detroit and had become the Lions. Newcomer Cincinnati couldn't handle pro football, losing its first eight games and being suspended for defaulting on its payment to the league. The Lions were garnished in NFL lore when their Thanksgiving Day game against Chicago was the first broadcast nationally by NBC. The Bears also joined the archives when rookie Beattie Feathers became the NFL's first 1,000-yard rusher with an astounding 1,004 yards on only 101 carries. However, it didn't carry into the championship game on December 9 on an icy field as the Giants defeated the Bears, 30–13.

There was a feeling of security among the owners the next two years despite the gathering war clouds in Europe. Germany took over the Saar from France in 1935, while months later, Italy invaded Ethiopia. Germany continued its aggression in 1936 by absorbing the Rhineland, a demilitarized area. Hitler also took pride later in June when Max Schmeling knocked out Joe Louis in the twelfth round. It didn't compare to what Jesse Owens did in the Berlin Olympics. He was the international star with four gold medals who was ignored by Hitler. Americans didn't ignore Roosevelt, who easily won a second term.

The NFL made a monumental decision in 1935. The owners endorsed Commissioner Bert Bell's proposal to begin an annual college draft in 1936. Designed to produce competitive balance, the teams would select players in an inverse order of finish invoking a passage in the Bible that "the last shall finish first." The Giants returned to the 1935 championship game for the second straight time but lost to the Lions, 26–7. The following season, the owners were sheltered by the fact that there weren't any franchise transactions for the first time since the formation of the league. Yet poor attendance continued to plague Boston. George Preston Marshall moved the championship game from Boston to New York's Polo Grounds, where the Packers and their sensational rookie, Don Hutson, ambushed the Braves 21–6.

By 1937 Marshall had enough of Boston. He moved the team out of the city and renamed them the Redskins in Washington. Marshall had the last laugh. With rookie quarterback Sammy Baugh leading the way, he brought a championship to the nation's capital when the Redskins defeated the Bears, 28–21. Life was improving in a country emerging from the Depression as Americans were singing two popular Rodgers and Hart songs, "My Funny Valentine" and "The Lady Is a Tramp," as Benny Goodman and his band took the nation by storm.

By 1938 the jobless rate had dwindled to eight million. FDR increased the minimum wage to forty cents an hour. On June 15 Cincinnati's Johnny Vander Meer pitched a second consecutive no-hitter, while a week later Joe Louis destroyed Max Schmeling with a first-round knockout at 2:04. With a championship, George Preston Marshall began to make his presence felt even more. He arranged with the *Los Angeles Times* to establish a Pro Bowl between the NFL champion and a team comprised of the league's all-stars beginning in January 1939. Another sensational rookie, Byron "Whizzer" White, who years later would be appointed to the U.S. Supreme Court, led the NFL in rushing as the Giants trimmed the Packers, 23–17, for the championship.

Germany continued its onslaught by taking over Czechoslovakia in 1939, and, for the first time, the Nazi Party made its presence known in the United States. A group numbering 22,000 held a rally in Madison Square Garden, prompting Hitler's nephew, William, to call him a "menace." Yet the World's Fair opened on schedule on April 30 in New York. Two days later, Yankee fans were saddened as Lou Gehrig's streak of 2,130 games ended. The NFL opened its season on an ominous note. Germany invaded Poland on September 30, and the next day England and France declared war. While the fair was taking place in New York and attracting thousands of visitors daily, the first NFL game was televised by NBC in nearby Brooklyn.

Although it didn't generate anywhere near the attention the World's Fair received, it would have far greater pertinent success for the NFL and the financial impact of television in the future. It didn't matter whether the Dodgers or the Eagles won; the game would have a bigger crowd than the paltry approximate number of 1,000 television sets. Television, a viable financial vault for the NFL, was beginning to seriously focus on pro football as a bona fide TV vehicle, especially since the league exceeded a total of over a million fans, an impressive 1,071,200. The Giants and Packers met for the championship for the second straight year, but this time Green Bay prevailed in Milwaukee, 27–0. However, the Giants did nip the Pro All-Stars in the Pro Bowl in Los Angeles, 13–10.

In the summer of 1940, German troops marched into Paris. The war was getting closer to America. By the fall, the first military draft spread across the nation, which had now incurred a $43 billion debt. Radio entered the NFL world. The Mutual Broadcasting System paid $2,500 for the right to air to 120 stations for the first time the league championship. George Halas incorporated Clark Shaughnessy of Stanford as an aide, and the results were overwhelming. Chicago destroyed Washington, 73–0, which was by far the most decisive championship victory in the league's existence. Looking to expand the NFL's popularity, the league's poobahs reached out to Notre Dame coach Elmer Layden in 1941 and made him the sport's first commissioner and moved its offices to Chicago, where the Bears continued their dominance. They finished deadlocked for the Western Division title with the Packers and defeated them in the first divisional playoff game, 33–14. They were even more dominant in the title game, humiliating the Giants, 37–9.

World War II cast its veil over the league just when it outgrew its adolescent years on its growth to maturation and fan acceptance. As the war grew nearer, Joe Louis retained his title with a seventh-round disqualification of Jimmy Braddock. On July 2 Joe DiMaggio hit in a record forty-five straight games, reaching fifty-six before he was stopped. On December 7, the Japanese forces destroyed Pearl Harbor on a day Roosevelt predicted would "live in infamy." The next day America was at war.

By the time 1942 ended, the United States had built 488 Liberty ships, entering a war on two sides of the globe. In rapid succession in March, the government had interned 100,000 Japanese Americans in California, the Philippines fell to Japan, and General Douglas MacArthur became the Supreme Commander of the Allied forces in the South Pacific. A month later, Air Force General James Doolittle led a squadron of B-25s on a surprise lightning raid on Japan. By June the U.S. completed its military leadership as General Dwight Eisenhower assumed command of U.S. forces in Europe. Pro football players leaving for the service depleted the talent in the league. Even the venerable George Halas left midway through the season to join the Navy, leaving Hunk Anderson, another Notre Dame product, to lead the Bears to an undefeated, 11–0, season. However, Sammy Baugh and his band of Redskins denied them the NFL title with a tightly contested 14–6 victory. The owners constituted a rule for the 1943 season that made the wearing of helmets mandatory for whatever talent that remained to contribute to a diminished ten-game schedule as players were distributed among the teams. Baugh continued to star, leading the league in passing, punting, and interceptions to help alleviate the shortage of legitimate professional personnel. Slingin' Sammy had it all. Baugh carried Washington to a tie for the Eastern title, then led the Redskins to a convincing 28–0 subjugation in the playoff game against the Giants. Not bad for a twangy-voiced cowboy from Texas. However, like a bride jilted at the altar, the Bears interrupted the ceremony with a raucous 42–21 win to avenge last year's loss to the same Redskins.

Change continued in the NFL and beyond to the dinner table in 1944. Canned goods, coffee, and sugar were rationed, along with meat and cheese, as FDR froze prices and wages to control inflation. The war front brightened. In 1943 General George Patton became the country's newest hero when his army captured Sicily in only thirty-eight days. The early months of 1944 brought even more security. MacArthur began his drive through the Pacific. U.S. marines and soldiers stormed beaches, freed islands, and raised America's hopes. Allied forces landed on Normandy, and U.S. planes bombed Berlin for the first time. Roosevelt easily won a fourth term after accepting his party's nomination by remarking, "I have as little right as a soldier to leave his position on the line."

During the war, the Cleveland Rams resumed operations in the NFL, and Ted Collins restored pro football in Boston with the name Yanks, while the Brooklyn Dodgers changed their stripes to Tigers. The paucity of players in 1943 necessitated the Eagles and Steelers to merge for one year under the innocuous banner of the Phil-Pitt Steagles, with the union dissolving the final day of the season. The Steelers then merged with the Chicago Cardinals for the 1944 season. Nevertheless, the Packers emerged victorious in 1944 with a 14–7 decision over the Giants.

Allied forces in Europe were also winning, and the reality of peace was imminent, so much so that the Big Three—Roosevelt, Winston Churchill, and Joseph Stalin—met in Yalta on February 11, 1945, much to the chagrin of Charles de Gaulle, who wasn't invited. Later that month, on February 23, the Stars and Stripes were raised over the island of Iwo Jima after four days of bitter fighting. A month later, Patton and his tanks crossed the Rhine on pontoon bridges that were built in forty-eight hours. Sadly for the world, Roosevelt unexpectedly died at sixty-three from a cerebral hemorrhage, and Harry Truman assumed occupancy of the Oval Office. Two other notable deaths followed. On April 28 Mussolini was killed, and two days later, Hitler committed suicide. A week later, Germany tendered its unconditional surrender. After an atomic bomb destroyed Hiroshima and Nagasaki on August 6 and 9, Japan called it quits a week later. There was one more sad death for Americans in 1945. On December 21 Patton died at age sixty in an Army hospital in Heidelberg from injuries sustained in a car wreck.

The league still felt the throes of the war in 1945, but it managed to continue. Halas rejoined the Bears late in the season in time to see an emerging new star. Rookie quarterback Bob Waterfield was the catalyst in Cleveland's 15–14 victory over Washington for the NFL championship. Besides Halas, there were 638 players who were called into service, with 21 of them never returning.

Nobody could anticipate what 1946 would bring. The war years severely infringed on the league's progression. Changes were dictated, and the variables began with the replacement of Commissioner Elmer Layden with Bert Bell. The first thing Bell did was to relocate the league's offices from Chicago to Philadelphia, if Bala-Cynwyd, a suburb of the city, could be spelled correctly without difficulty. Despite Bala-whatever, the NFL unequivocally took on a national reflection for truly the first time when Cleveland owner Dan Reeves was granted permission to move his champions to Los Angeles as an enticement for Waterfield and his sultry actress-wife, Jane Russell. In a sense, the NFL was going Hollywood. Reeves continued his Tinsel Town makeup by signing UCLA stars halfback Kenny Washington and end Woody Strode, who became the first African Americans to play in the modern era of the NFL.

There was still unrest in America. On January 27 some 800,000 steelworkers joined millions of others on strike. That same month the United Nations held its first session in London. In March Winston Churchill, in a speech in Fulton, Missouri, warned the world that "an iron curtain has descended across the continent." On June 19 Joe Louis knocked out Billy Conn in the eighth round of their rematch. Twice was enough for Conn, who announced, "I'm quitting. This is my last fight." It was almost the last of the supplies of standard meats, which had reached a record low, as New Yorkers began eating horse meat.

Still, the All-America Football Conference began play with eight teams and the coming of Paul Brown in Cleveland, who won the first championship of many he would achieve in making the Browns a legitimate power in the years ahead. In a close game, the Browns nipped the New York Yankees, 14–9. Meanwhile, a potential scandal reared its ugly head in the NFL. Giants quarterback Frankie Filchock and running back Merle Hapes were interrogated concerning a bribe they were offered to fix the championship game. Hapes was suspended, but Bell allowed Filchock to play as the Bears won, 24–14.

Branch Rickey shocked the baseball world in 1947 when he made second baseman Jackie Robinson the first African American to play in the major leagues. Henry Ford, who put America on wheels, died at eighty-three. On May 29 the worst air disaster in U.S. history occurred in New York. A United Airlines plane, with forty-four passengers on board, burst into flames just after take-off from LaGuardia Airport. Meanwhile, Jack Kramer brought back some respect for America's tennis world when he became the first American to win at Wimbledon since Bobby

Riggs in 1939. The Browns repeated as AAFC champions as the Cardinals won the NFL crown, 28–21, over the Eagles, who had blanked Pittsburgh the week before in a playoff, 21–0.

Strikes were still around in 1948. On March 5 200,000 miners went on strike for better pensions. Eisenhower said farewell to the military with rumors abounding that he would be a presidential candidate. In May the state of Israel came into existence. Citation, with Eddie Arcaro aboard, won the Triple Crown, and a month later Leo Durocher resigned as manager of the Dodgers and became the same with the heated rival Giants across the river. In August, the United States came away with thirty-eight medals at the London Olympics. But the biggest news of the year was Harry Truman's confounding the political experts by winning the presidency over Thomas E. Dewey and embarrassing a Chicago newspaper that prematurely printed a headline proclaiming Dewey the winner.

The upstart Browns raised eyebrows with a third consecutive championship with an authoritarian performance in 1948. They swept through an unbeaten 14–0 season and then annihilated the Buffalo Bills, 49–7, for the title. They were every bit a juggernaut as Patton and his tank corps in the war that ended. All the NFL could offer for its championship game was a blizzard and a paltry 7–0 win by the Eagles over the Cardinals. By now, the league had recognized the Browns as a worthy and dangerous adversary.

While the Browns were arriving as a football power, another champion, Joe Louis, left boxing on March 1, 1949, after holding the title of champ for over eleven years. That fall, Egypt and Israel ended their war with the signing of an armistice on the island of Rhodes, where Greek mythology had flourished centuries earlier. Sam Snead won the Masters in April, and a month later the Berlin blockade ended. On August 16 a heartbreaking life ended in Atlanta. Margaret Mitchell, author of the classic *Gone with the Wind,* was instantly killed when hit by a speeding motorist. And in only his second year in the major leagues, Jackie Robinson won the batting title and was named the National League's Most Valuable Player.

While the NFL continued to build its star power in competition with the AAFC, league owners grew more concerned with the Browns. In 1949 the older league produced two 1,000-yard rushers in the same season for the first time. One was quarterback Steve Van Buren of the Eagles, who was a bona fide triple threat, and the other was Tony Canadeo of the Packers. On December 9, two days before the AAFC championship game, Bell announced that the Cleveland Browns, Baltimore Colts, and San Francisco 49ers would join the NFL in 1950, which meant the end of the rival consortium. It was business as usual for the Browns, who routinely took their fourth consecutive championship by defeating the 49ers, 21-7. A week later, the Eagles kept their wings dry by shutting out the Rams in a heavy rainstorm, 14-0, to win the NFL championship.

Television began to emerge as a force in pro football the following two years. The Rams became the first NFL team to have all of their games, home and away, televised. George Preston Marshall was quick to follow. The Redskins endorsed a contract to televise their games, while other teams contracted for selected games to be shown. The Browns were still a devastating legion their first year in the NFL and showed it by defeating the Rams, 30-28, for the 1950 crown. Unfortunately, the league suffered a setback when Baltimore couldn't prosper under the NFL banner and was forced to disband.

The Browns were again back in the championship game in 1951 in a repeat meeting with the Rams. The game was televised nationally for the first time by the DuMont Network, which paid the NFL a stipend of $75,000. However, the Browns didn't repeat as champions, losing to the Rams, 24–17. In 1952 the NFL experienced a bizarre setback. A new group in Dallas was awarded a franchise, only to return it to the league at midseason. The commissioner's office assumed the role of caretaker and operated the Texans as a road team the last five games of the season, using Hershey, Pennsylvania, as a home base, yet not even posing a threat to the tourism the Hershey Chocolate factory generated. In what was beginning to appear monotonous, the Browns were once again in the championship game, but stumbled to Detroit, 17–7. Although Paul Brown couldn't care less, his team provided the Lions with their first bunting in seventeen years, so the points were indeed symbolic.

Baseball was still the most popular sport when the 1950s arrived, as evidenced by Boston's Ted Williams signing a record $125,000 contract. (Almost ten years earlier, just before he went into the service after the 1941 season, the Splendid Splinter led all of baseball with a .406 average and was acknowledged as the best pure hitter in the game.) The country's worst strike of 1950 was the two-month-old coal walkout, which was finally settled on March 5. By June Ben Hogan had recovered from a near-fatal car accident to win the U.S. Open. Another hero, General Douglas MacArthur, was also busy, as he was named to head the UN forces in Korea on July 8. The following month, a new hero emerged in the sports world. Althea Gibson, a twenty-two-year-old from Harlem, became the first African American to compete in the U.S. Open tennis championship. Two weeks later Americans cheered twenty-four-year-old Florence Chadwick of California on her record swim of thirteen hours, twenty minutes across the English Channel.

By 1951 drive-in movies were the rage. The number of outdoor screens doubled to 2,200. On October 18 the amazing eighty-seven-year-old Connie Mack retired as manager of the Philadelphia Athletics, as President Truman reassured voters that the United States would avoid incursion into China. Eisenhower surfaced in the news again after being named commander of NATO's forces. On Christmas Day, Sugar Ray Robinson ended a successful five-victory European tour with four knockouts.

The atomic age rumbled into the headlines in 1951. An atomic test in Nevada, 45 miles from Las Vegas, rattled the Southwest. So did Sugar Ray Robinson on February 14. The welterweight king stepped up in class and took away Jake LaMotta's middleweight crown with a thirteenth-round TKO. On July 10 Randy Turpin upset Robinson to take his crown back to England. In a rematch two months later, Robinson snatched his title back with a tenth-round knockout. Former heavyweight champion Joe Louis attempted a comeback on October 26 but was knocked out by Rocky Marciano in the eighth round. In the political arena Truman relieved MacArthur of his command, but that didn't prevent New Yorkers from giving the war hero a triumphal Broadway parade.

The first public statement by Ike regarding a run for the presidency appeared on January 7, 1952, when he said that he would accept the Republican party's nomination if he was asked. In July it became official, with the Republican ticket of Ike and Richard Nixon. The same month, Argentina's beloved Eva Peron died at thirty-three. On September 23 Marciano knocked out thirty-eight-year-old Jersey Joe Walcott in the thirteenth round. Ike and Nixon had a bigger one in November with a landslide victory over Adlai Stevenson for the White House. Vending machines, the newest convenience craze, had its biggest year, grossing $1.25 billion.

Frozen food sales in 1953 rivaled vending machines with a billion dollars in sales. Joseph Stalin died in Moscow at seventy-three, weeks before the Salk vaccine was used successfully against the ravages of polio. Marciano was active and a popular champion. On May 15 he knocked out Walcott again in a return title match and on September 24 disposed of Roland La Starza with an eleven-round TKO. Ernest Hemingway was also a big winner, nominated for a Pulitzer for his novella *The Old Man and the Sea.* The biggest social event of the year was the Newport, Rhode Island, wedding of John F. Kennedy and Jacqueline Lee Bouvier, as a crowd of 3,000 tried to crash the affair.

The NFL was determined to have a franchise in Baltimore in 1953 and found a willing owner in Carroll Rosenbloom. League officials even helped him get started by awarding him the assets of the defunct Dallas organization on January 23, although there wasn't much player value in whatever assets there were. The team was called the Colts, and they found enough marketable players (five) to acquire ten from Cleveland in the largest trade in NFL history. However, the players Cleveland acquired from Baltimore in the trade apparently weren't much help, as the Browns again lost to the Lions, 17–16, in the championship game.

The Canadian Football League ambitiously crossed the border in 1954 with a series of raids on the NFL teams. Among the notables they returned with were quarterback Eddie LeBaron and defensive end Gene Brito from Washington and defensive tackle Arnie Weinmeister of the Giants. The CFL failed to land fullback Joe Perry of the 49ers, who became the first player to accumulate consecutive 1,000-yard seasons. Cleveland was a familiar figure in the championship game; this time they avenged last year's 1-point loss to Detroit by easily caging the Lions, 56–10.

It was a comeback year for singer Frank Sinatra, who won an Oscar for his role in *From Here to Eternity.* England's Roger Bannister became the first to break the four-minute mile with a time of 3:59:4. Marciano continued to rule the boxing world with a fifteenth-round decision over Ezzard Charles on June 17. Ike established the Air Force Academy in Colorado on April 1, and two weeks later 3,000 troops returned from Korea. They would see television in a different light, as RCA began producing 12-inch color TV sets for under $1,000. In a historical day in the automotive industry, on November 23, GM produced its fifty millionth car.

Economic progress allowed the AFL and CIO to merge in the early part of 1955, as Tennessee Williams's *Cat on a Hot Tin Roof* opened on Broadway on March 24. A month later, Churchill retired at age eighty but still maintained his ever-present cigar. The same month, on April 18, physicist Albert Einstein died in Princeton, New Jersey. On July 18 America and the world were introduced to Disneyland, which debuted in Anaheim, California, just two weeks after Johnny Carson made his entrance into television on CBS. Leo Durocher, who had managed the Giants since 1948, resigned. The nation's teenagers were saddened by the death of twenty-four-year-old screen idol James Dean, who was killed in a car accident ten days before the Dodgers won their first World Series by beating the Yankees in the seventh game, 2–0.

In what didn't appear to be significant at the time, sudden death overtime was seen for the first time in an NFL preseason game between the Giants and Rams in Portland, Oregon. Three minutes into the extra period, the Rams came away with a 6-point victory, 23–17. When the regular season ended, the Rams also appeared in the championship game but absorbed a 38–14 beating by Cleveland. Browns quarterback Otto Graham played his final game with a phenomenal accomplishment. He had led the Browns to ten championship appearances in ten years. It was an auspicious beginning for NBC, which had replaced DuMont as the title game network for $100,000.

For seven years, the biggest bank robbery in America was still unsolved. However, on January 12, 1956, the FBI finally identified the men behind the $2.7 billion Brinks Robbery in Boston. On February 29 Autherine Lucy took a Giants leap for civil rights when she became the first African American to attend the University of Alabama. The event was so huge that lawyer Thurgood Marshall remarked, "That girl sure has guts." Martin Luther King Jr. wasn't so fortunate in Alabama. On March 22 he was found guilty of orchestrating the Montgomery bus riots. Boxing lost its biggest attraction when Rocky Marciano, unbeaten in forty-seven fights in which he resisted forty-three knockouts, retired on April 19. Two big weddings were newsmakers. Actress Grace Kelly and the Prince of Monaco were married in Monaco on April 19. Two months later, actress Marilyn Monroe and playwright Arthur Miller did the same in London. In November, in another landslide victory, Ike was reelected president.

Perhaps the first weighty sign that the NFL was becoming a viable entity also occurred in 1956, with the formation of the National Football League Players Association. Not only did it provide solidarity for the players, but in the years ahead it would become a powerful bargaining force with management. CBS detected as much and became the first network to broadcast a number of games to selected television markets across America. The Giants, emerging as a power, overwhelmed the Bears for the championship, 47–7, which prompted George Halas to retire yet again. It was also the year that unknown Johnny Unitas entered the league.

Two prominent deaths within two days in the entertainment field ushered in 1957. Movie star Humphrey Bogart died of cancer in Los Angeles, and on January 16, Arturo Toscanini passed away in New York. In March the FBI arrested the teamsters' Jimmy Hoffa on bribery charges, while ten days later, on

March 22, San Francisco suffered its worst earthquake since the killer one in 1906. Althea Gibson won Wimbledon and was given a parade from New York's City Hall to her home in Harlem. Ike gave the country a scare on November 26 by suffering a mild stroke.

Rams public relations director Pete Rozelle was elevated to general manager and would become involved in league matters that would ultimately lead to his meteoric rise as commissioner three years later, in 1960. It was an exciting year for the NFL, as a record crowd of 102,368 attended the San Francisco–Los Angeles game on November 1 at the Coliseum. It came three weeks too late for 49er owner Tony Morabito, who succumbed to a heart attack in his box during a game against the Bears in Kezar Stadium. The Lions captured the attention of pro football fans, first by roaring back from a 20-point deficit to steal a 31–27 playoff win over the 49ers, then by going on to destroy the Browns for the championship, 59–14.

Yet it could never equal what would happen in 1958.

THE GIANTS

A $500 Bookmaker's Team

Few, if any, fans knew the origin of the Giants. The team joined the league in 1925, two years after it was formed—if one could call outfits in Kenosha, Rochester, Dayton, Pottsville, and Columbus a major professional football amalgamation. For the shaky league to survive, it needed exposure, and there was no better place than New York. The Giants neophyte owner, Tim Mara, was a successful businessman and, of all things, a respected bookmaker. Back then, bookmaking was legal, and Mara felt no guilt attending Mass on Sundays, arm and arm with his family, on Manhattan's Upper West Side.

Mara's resolve brought professional football to New York. The league of pioneers, who had been treading water since 1920, wasn't exactly a prudent model of stability and financial dividends. As it turned out decades later, Mara made a wise investment in 1925 when he plunked down $500 cash to join the aspiring league. He had friends in high places, and the money he handed over was nothing more than covering a bet to him.

Mara had no intention of buying a professional football team that spring. Being a sportsman, he would spend most of his day at the racetrack or the nearby Polo Grounds to watch his beloved Giants and their Irish manager, fiery John McGraw. Down deep, he was a promoter. He'd promote anything that touched his Irish soul.

What he really wanted was to own a fighter. He was enthralled with Gene Tunney, the light-heavyweight champion of the world. He approached Tunney's manager, Billy Gibson, about buying out his contract. Gibson refused but suggested that Mara would be better off in the long run by getting into pro football. Decades later, Mara mentioned to a writer that "I figured an empty store in New York was worth five hundred dollars."

In essence he knew everything about New York but nothing about football, yet he was convinced that there was a market for the sport in Gotham. Besides, being a gambling man, $500 was chump change. He was well known around town, with close ties to the politicians and the sports stars, as well as with his clientele, who would legally bet with him at the racetrack. Mara was a handsome man who dressed well, with a trademark black derby hat. He was well liked, with his Irish smile, and dined in the city's best restaurants. But football, well, that was some-thing else. It was new to him, so new that he stuck with the same Giants' name for his football team.

Mara didn't wait long to invoke his promotional acumen. After basking in New York's nightlife of show people and celeb-rities, he realized that marquee players would translate into ticket sales, and he found such a big one in Rock Island, Illinois. Olympic hero and everybody's All-American Jim Thorpe wasn't happy playing for the local Independents. Mara brought him to New York and had him signed within an hour. Thorpe was thirty-seven years old and nowhere near the great player he had been. But his name was still valuable, and New Yorkers, whether in the entertainment world or the sports arena, would respond to a legend like Thorpe.

Unfortunately, age had caught up with Thorpe in 1925, and coupled with a knee injury, he lasted only three games with the Giants, losing all of them. It was the Giants defense that dominated the headlines in producing shutouts in the next four games. They put together a seven-game winning streak when they lined up against the Bears December 6 at the Polo Grounds. Mara's star theory was dramatically displayed by the presence of Chicago's Red Grange, who had achieved legendary status at Illinois. It was Grange who attracted not only 70,000 fans but also the renowned sportswriters of the time. Grantland Rice, Damon Runyon, Westbrook Pegler, and Paul Gallico occupied seats in the press box. Grange contributed a touchdown with an interception in the Bears 19–7 victory before the largest crowd to see a professional football game, and for Mara it helped cut his financial losses that first year.

"It rained all week before the game," related Mara. "Still, we had $100,000 in the till in advance. I have never known so great a demand for tickets. Hundreds scaled the walls and rushed the gates, and we had to seat many important people along the sidelines because the stands were sold out."

The Bears and Giants met again in the season's final game the following week in Chicago and the Giants won 9–0. Mara was happy with an 8–4 record.

The Giants had another winning season in 1926, winning five of their last six games to finish 8–4–1. Yet their success on the field didn't translate to the box office. Mara also had competition from promoter C. C. Pyle and Grange the following year. They were granted a franchise in Yankee Stadium for the 1927 season and called themselves the Yankees, which didn't sit well with the Giants owner, who nevertheless enjoyed pleasure from his team's performance. With a ferocious defense led by powerful Cal Hubbard, the Giants surrendered only 20 points in thirteen games, a record never equaled in the league, and won their first championship with an 11–1–1 record, clinching it with a tough 13–7 triumph over the Bears. Giants tackle Steve Owen, who would later coach the Giants for twenty-three years, affirmed the tenacious struggle with Chicago.

"It was the roughest, toughest game I ever played," waxed Owen, who played all sixty minutes opposite Jim McMillen. "When the gun went off, both of us sat on the ground in the middle of the field. We didn't say a word. We couldn't. He smiled in a tired way, reached over to me, and we shook hands. It was fully five minutes before we got up to go to the dressing room."

—

Mara had a big smile on his face all over town after the 1927 season, and it was there all the way into August, when he went on his annual trip to Saratoga, where he could be found every day at the historic racetrack. After being in the league only three years, his Giants had won their first championship. Still, he continued promoting fights, and he still harbored thoughts of owning Tunney after failing to purchase his contract two years earlier.

"The biggest bet my father ever made was on Gene Tunney," claimed his son Wellington. "He loved him. He knew absolutely nothing about football. He didn't even have a clue. I remember a game against Orange, New Jersey, a couple of years after he bought the team. One of our backs ran a sweep, cut back to avoid a tackler, then reversed himself again and ran in the original direction. My father was on his feet screaming and hollering. He looked down at me and said, 'What a great run.' I had to explain to him that, after all of that, the runner made only 3 yards."

The Giants were playing good football but still losing money from a blasé fan base. Governor Al Smith, a guest at Mara's home one evening, approached him about it.

"Pro football will never amount to anything!" declared Smith. "Why don't you give it up?"

"The boys would run me right out of the house if I did," smiled Mara.

Mara was thinking about another championship in 1928. However, he had a disgruntled team. Beset by money losses, Mara tightened the purse strings, much to the chagrin of the players, who even had to spend a night at the YMCA when they were in Chicago to play the Bears. The Giants went 4–7–2 with an anemic offense that averaged only 6 points a game. Mara had to do something, and he did, by getting rid of eighteen players.

Mara tried to generate interest by employing Chick Wergeles, a fight manager and publicist, to mine the newspapers for publicity. It didn't work.

"I toured the newspaper offices, offering a dozen tickets, two dozen, anything the guy wanted," explained Wergeles. "They didn't want much. You would think I was trying to sell dollar bills for ninety-eight cents. The Giants gave away three or four thousand tickets a game, if they could find that many, and only drew a few thousand paid. This was at two dollars and a buck a seat, while the colleges went as high as four dollars and even six sixty."

Mara wasn't finished either. In 1929 he made a monumental decision to acquire the talented quarterback Benny Friedman from the Detroit Wolverines. Although the franchise was financially troubled, Detroit stubbornly rebuffed Mara four separate times. Finally, with the guile of a champion bridge player, Mara bought the entire Detroit team and closed down the operation. Friedman, who was an artist with the football, as a passer, runner, and kicker, was worth the price in Mara's mind, and he was determined to get him. It was costly. Even Friedman realized it.

"I was paid $10,000 a year," remarked Friedman. "It was an exorbitant amount of money when considering the highest paid player was only pocketing $125 a game."

Friedman was a handsome, intelligent athlete who would draw fans to the mossy Polo Grounds. In high school, one of his coaches told him he would never be a football player. When he graduated from Michigan, Benny was a hot commodity. He was not only an accurate passer but also an elusive runner and could boot extra points. Friedman had a knack for freezing the defense by faking a run with the ball held high in his hands as he got near the line of scrimmage, only to throw a pass, and he played the game with passion.

Mara's investment reaped dividends. Friedman led the Giants to an impressive 13–1–1 record. The only loss was against unbeaten Green Bay, 20-6. Benny was the talk of New York with his nineteen touchdown passes, three times more than any other passer.

It was a big reason why the Giants were seen as title contenders in 1930. They looked every bit the part with an eight-game winning streak and a 10-1 record in November. However, they unexpectedly stumbled in their final five games, losing two of them, and finished 13-4. Friedman had another banner year, with a league-leading fourteen touchdown passes and another seven rushing, second best overall.

Mara came up with another brainstorm. He met with Mayor Jimmy Walker and proposed a charity game between the Giants and a team of Notre Dame All-Stars coached by Knute Rockne to help New York's unemployed in the Great Depression. Even though the December weather was extremely cold, 55,000 diehards, lured by Notre Dame's fabled Four Horsemen, braved the elements. Rockne realized he would need a miracle to pull off a win. Before the game, he stopped by the Giants locker room.

"Rockne wasn't well at the time and walked in with a cane," remembered Friedman, who was getting his ankles taped. "He was one of my idols and I said, 'Hi, Coach.'"

"Hello, Benny," replied Rockne.

"What can I do for you?" asked Friedman.

"I think we ought to cut the quarters to ten minutes."

"Oh, Lord, we can't do that. There are some 50,000 people out there. If it gets bad, we'll cut it down in the second half. Anything else?"

"Yeah, for Pete's sake, take it easy."

Benny did, as the Giants blanked the Irish, 22–0, and it could have been worse. A day later, Mara handed Mayor Walker a check for $115,153.

•

The Giants struggled financially their first five years in the league, and when the stock market crashed, Mara didn't have any time for football. Yet he still had intense passion for the Giants and was firm in his belief that pro football could make it in New York. He kept the Giants viable with financial aid from his other enterprises and looked to his sons, Jack and Wellington, to look after the team. Overnight, Wellington, only fourteen years old at the time, became the youngest owner of a professional football team. That left George Halas, one of the founders of the league in Chicago, looking with trepidation toward New York.

The Giants slumped to fifth place in 1931 with a 7–6–1 performance in the first year of Steve Owen's long tenure as head coach. It also marked the signing of center Mel Hein, who would anchor the offensive line for the next fifteen years. Friedman left the Giants before the 1932 season after asking for a piece of the team along with his salary. Mara wouldn't consider it. It wasn't a good year. When it ended, the Giants were in fifth place (4–6–2).

With the stock market demise behind him and the football team shaky, Mara went back to promoting fights. It was the Irish in him. In 1932 he promoted one of the biggest fights in the city, Jimmy McLarnin against Lou Brouillard in Yankee Stadium. In 1933 he scored with two heavyweight fights. The first was Max Schmeling against Max Baer, followed by Jack Sharkey against Primo Carnera. The Schmeling–Baer fight attracted 60,000 fans in Yankee Stadium. Coincidentally, the referee that night was Art Donovan, whose son, Art, would play against the Giants in the 1958 championship game.

Getting Ken Strong gave the Giants the best backfield in the NFL in 1933 and had both Mara and Owen optimistically looking at a championship. After a month, it didn't appear that way, as the Giants went 2–2 before going on a rampage after a berating from Owen. They lost only one other time, finished 11–3, and faced Chicago in the first NFL championship game in Wrigley Field. The Giants were ahead, 21–16, in the closing minutes when the Bears pushed over the winning touchdown, 23–21. New York had a final chance to score but was stopped on a game-saving tackle by Red Grange.

The Giants started slowly in 1934, losing their first two games before going on a five-game winning streak. They then lost to the Bears before facing them again two weeks later at the Polo Grounds. The crowd of 55,000 brought joy to Mara's face but when the game ended it was gone. A last minute field goal gave Chicago a 10–9 win.

With an 8–5 record, the Giants nevertheless won the Eastern Division and encountered their nemesis, the Bears, who were 10–2–1 for the championship on a bitter cold December afternoon at the Polo Grounds. The temperature was barely above zero, which left the playing field a sheet of ice as some 46,000 fans sat bundled in their seats. End Ray Flaherty approached Owen before the game. "Why don't we wear sneakers?" he suggested. "When I was playing for Gonzaga, we did that once on a frozen field. We borrowed them from our basketball team and went out and beat a team that was a lot better than us."

Where could the Giants possibly find sneakers? It was Sunday, and stores in New York were closed. Besides, it was so cold, nothing was moving around the city. Yet Owen came up with an idea that could work.

"We had a little fellow on the payroll named Abe Cohen, a sort of jack-of-all trades," recalled Wellington Mara. "Abe was a tailor by profession, but he also worked for Coach Chick Meehan at Manhattan College, which was nearby. Owen asked Abe to go there and borrow the sneakers from the lockers of the basketball players. He got back with nine or ten pairs."

When Cohen returned after the third quarter, he found the Bears ahead, 13–3. Ken Strong laced up one of the sneakers and proceeded to run wild past the sliding defenders who approached him. He scored two touchdowns as the Giants scored 27 points for a 30–13 triumph.

Mara accompanied the team to the West Coast, the beginning of a barnstorming tour designed to promote the league. He never saw the game. Two days after the team arrived in California, he surprised the players by telling them that he was returning to New York. He told center Mel Hein that he had trouble sleeping, and the birds chirping early in the morning didn't help any.

"Tim said he needed to go to New York, where he could hear the subway and the fire engines and all the racket, because the quiet was driving him crazy," disclosed Hein. "He couldn't sleep unless he heard all the noises of New York."

The Giants won the division for the third straight time in 1935. They finished 9–3, while Detroit took the West with a 7–3–2 slate. They met for the title in Detroit. An inclement day limited the crowd to 15,000. The Lions took the opening kickoff, roared for a touchdown, and never looked back in a 26–7 victory. Only Strong's 42-yard touchdown reception prevented a shutout.

During the 1935 season, Wellington took the first game films the Giants ever had with a bulky Bell and Howell camera that he had received for his birthday. He'd have the film developed overnight for viewing the next morning

"I knew all our plays, so I knew where the ball was going," he confessed rather sheepishly. "The other cameraman knew little about football and nothing about our team. I knew what the coach wanted."

The next year Wellington began scouting college games on Saturday. He was meticulous in compiling files not only on the players he observed that day but also on others throughout the country. It was no wonder that his father and his brother, Jack, felt secure in the football arena.

"We had no scouting budget," said Wellington. "I would buy all the college football magazines and subscribe to a whole bunch of out-of-town newspapers."

In the next two years the Giants failed to reach the championship game. Strong left after the 1936 season. But the Giants had a promising newcomer in Tuffy Leemans to replace him. The year before, Wellington, who was nineteen at the time, pleaded with his father to allow him to go to Washington to recruit Leemans. Tim told him to do it.

"I sent a telegram setting up a meeting and signed my father's name to it," confessed Wellington. "When I got there, he thought I was a kid who wanted his autograph. He said he was meeting Tim Mara, the owner of the Giants. I was able to convince him who I was, and we got him for the Giants."

If it weren't for Leemans, the Giants might not have even gone 5–6–1. He led the NFL in rushing with 830 yards and made All-Pro as a rookie.

Fans needed a program to identify the Giants in 1937. In the large transformation, seventeen rookies were on the twenty-five-man roster. They performed well, producing a 6–3–2 campaign. The team's financial records looked better, too. The Giants attracted 260,000 fans in seven home games and closed their books in the black. Mara couldn't have been happier.

After a surprisingly solid season, the young Giants appeared primed for 1938. For the second straight year, they were in a battle with Washington for the East crown. The youthful Giants were 7–2–1 and the Redskins 6–2–2 when they met at the Polo Grounds. It was no contest. New York thumped Washington, 36–0, for the title and a date with Green Bay for the championship.

The largest crowd to view an NFL title game, 48,120, was in attendance in New York. With Leemans scoring one of the touchdowns, the Giants had a slim 16–14 halftime edge. A third-quarter field goal gave the Packers a 17–16 lead. However, the Giants bounced right back and scored what eventually was the winning touchdown to culminate a 61-yard drive, 23–17.

As the decade of the '30s was nearing its end, Mara emerged as one of the NFL's power brokers. He took his place alongside Halas and Redskins owner George Preston Marshall, the shepherds of a league that was still finding its way. Professional football was beginning to grow roots in the league's three biggest cities, which allowed Halas and Marshall to devise a blueprint that divided the circuit into two four-team divisions, the Eastern and the Western.

For the third consecutive year, the Giants and Redskins continued their rivalry for Eastern supremacy. New York's defense was exemplary the first six games, allowing an average of 6½ points a game. When the Giants and Redskins met once again in the final game of the season at the Polo Grounds, both teams were 8–1–1. Despite the rain, over 62,000 faithful showed up. On a muddy field, offense would be at a premium. After three quarters, all the scoring, 9–0, was the result of three Giants field goals. Washington scored the game's only touchdown in the fourth quarter and almost pulled out a victory on a field goal attempt that was missed.

The 9–2 Packers waited for the Giants in Wisconsin for the championship joust. The wait was rewarded. New York was never in the game, and when it finally concluded, they failed to score a point in a 27–0 debacle, the most lopsided score in championship competition.

●

By 1939, when he had graduated from college, Wellington had come full circle. He was given the responsibility of running the college draft for the club. The move was not lost on NFL Commissioner Bert Bell.

"The success of the Giants is their organization," remarked Bell. "Tim Mara is a smart businessman, Jack Mara is a great executive, and there is that damn little Wellington. Nobody ever beats him on some unknown player who can be a star, and he won't take a well-known player if he feels that man won't produce. The little son-of-a-gun is never wrong."

Jack was in law school at Fordham when Tim instructed him to run the Giants from the business side. The brothers had a harrowing challenge. New York was still a baseball metropolis, while college football was still king. With Jack on top at one end and young Wellington on the football sidelines, the brothers solidified the franchise.

There was no championship appearance for the Giants in 1940. There were several contributing factors. Quarterback Ed

Danowski retired, and Leemans was lost for the year midway through the season. None of the rookies were productive, and the Giants ended the year at 6–4–1.

However, they contended for the championship with an 8–3 outburst in 1941. Danowski came back from his retirement, and Leemans was fully recovered from his back injury. In their first five games, the rejuvenated Giants outscored their opponents, 122–27. The championship game against the Bears didn't attract much interest, and it was understandable. It was two weeks after the attack on Pearl Harbor, and only 13,341 fans showed up at Wrigley Field, accounting for the smallest number to watch an NFL championship game. The 10–4 Bears, who trailed 6–3 after the opening quarter, went on the prowl and clawed the Giants, 37–9.

＊

During the NFL's lean years, Mara, Halas, and Marshall were the vanguards who kept the league solvent. When World War II broke out, most of the owners wanted to disband until the conflict ended. However, it was Mara who lobbied for the game to continue despite the reality of the draft, which would absorb quite an amount of the league's players. Halas, himself, went into the Navy, as did Wellington. In the four years that America was at war, the Giants won two Eastern Division championships.

The war took its toll on the Giants, and the entire sports world in general. "I took one look at the squad and I felt like crying," remarked Leemans, who wasn't drafted because of his back. "It hurt to see the Giants I loved having as miserable a group as we had here." The Giants were fortunate to finish 1942 at 5–5–1.

In 1943 the league was reduced to nine teams, which forced the financially strapped Pittsburgh and Philadelphia teams to combine as the Pitt-Steagles. Mel Hein retired to take a coaching position upstate, but Owen pleaded with him to return to

New York on the weekends and play. "It wasn't easy," admitted Hein. "I had to play the full sixty minutes on the hottest day Boston ever had. What a toll it took. I could hardly get on a train to get to Schenectady that night. It took about three weeks to get rid of all that soreness. Still, the next week I had to go sixty minutes again."

A record crowd of 56,591 saw an amazing performance in the Polo Grounds on November 14. Chicago quarterback Sid Luckman put on a mind-boggling record performance, passing for seven touchdowns and 453 yards in a 56–7 rout. At 6–3–1, the Giants tied for the divisional crown but were blanked by the Redskins, 28–0.

The retirement of Leemans in 1944 prompted the Giants to talk thirty-four-year-old Packers quarterback Arnie Herber out of retirement. They went even further by bringing back thirty-eight-year-old Ken Strong, who had been out of the game since 1939. And thirty-five-year-old Mel Hein was still doing his weekend commute from Union College in Schenectady. It was a lot of age. The offense was built around running backs Bill Paschal and Ward Cuff. But the vanguard of the team was its defense. They forged an 8–1–1 season with five shutouts in outscoring the opposition, 206–75. Paschal led the league in rushing (737 yards), and Strong had enough strength left in his leg to kick the most field goals (six) and 23 of 24 extra points. Howie Livingston turned out to be a rookie sensation with nine interceptions, best in the league. Unfortunately, the Giants fell short of the championship on a 14–7 loss to Green Bay.

◦

The war ended, and nobody expected the Giants to do a complete reversal in 1945. Age surfaced as New York went 3–6–1, the fewest victories since they entered the league in 1925. Both Hein and Herber had enough and retired. (Tim Mara told a tale at Toots Shor's joint that Wellington returned from the Navy as a radar expert, and Owen was curious if Wellington's skill would help him decipher signals of the Bears and Redskins, in particular. He said it with tongue in cheek, but that's the way it was at Toots' place.)

The Giants got quarterback Frankie Filchock to lead them in 1946, and he indeed did, to a 7-3-1 Eastern championship. Filchock became the first in team history to pass for over 1,000 yards, with twelve touchdowns. He also led the ground game with 371 yards, as the Giants prepared to meet the Bears in the Polo Grounds for the big prize.

However, before they did so, they were sacked by a scandal that involved two of their star players, Filchock and running back Merle Hapes. It conjured memories of baseball's infamous Black Sox scandal. Commissioner Bert Bell informed Mara that a gambler named Alvin Paris offered both players $2,500 each to dump the game. Hapes confessed the bribe to Bell, but Filchock claimed he didn't know anything about the offer. However, he did acknowledge that he knew Paris. Bell suspended Hapes from playing because he didn't report Paris's offer but allowed Filchock to play. It was the final game he would ever play for the Giants, who were beaten, 24-14.

It didn't take long for the Giants to rid themselves of Filchock and Hapes, but it left them without a passer for the 1947 season. It showed, too. After an opening game deadlock, they lost seven straight games, which forced them after the fourth one to trade Paschal to Boston for Paul Governali, who was a star in college at Columbia. In the remaining eight games, Governali established two Giants records, throwing for 1,461 yards and fourteen touchdowns. But that was all the offense the Giants had, as they dropped into the cellar with the worst record, 2-8-2.

That was Governali's first and last season as a starter. In 1948 the Giants, fortunately, acquired Charlie Conerly from

Washington, who would remain the team's quarterback for the next fourteen years.

On the defensive side, they found a gem in Emlen Tunnell, who showed up at the Giants' training camp that summer and quietly asked for a tryout. Wellington Mara was impressed with Tunnell, who had recovered from a broken neck after playing only one year of college ball.

"If you have the guts to come in here and ask for a job, then I'm going to give you a chance," proposed Wellington.

Tunnell made the most of it and was a key part of the defense for the next eleven years. When he retired, he was regarded as perhaps the finest defensive back the league had ever seen and was selected to the Pro Football Hall of Fame.

Conerly set an NFL record of thirty-six completions against Pittsburgh and established team records of 2,175 passing yards, 162 completions, and 22 touchdowns. A porous defense, underlined by a 63–35 loss to the Chicago Cardinals, was the undoing of the Giants, who suffered through a 4–8 campaign.

A frustrated Steve Owen decided to junk his A formation in 1949 and switch to the standard T, which was a better fit for Conerly. The quarterback from Mississippi responded with 2,138 yards and seventeen touchdowns. End Bill Swiacki produced club marks with forty-seven catches and 652 yards. But Gene "Choo-Choo" Roberts was a favorite, as he led the NFL in scoring with 102 points and seventeen touchdowns to give the Giants a .500 season at 6–6.

It was the Giants defense that took them to the top in 1950. Owen had devised a 6-1-4 formation he called "The Umbrella," which was specifically effective against the pass. The Giants lost only two games, and their 10–2 record tied them with the Browns and created a playoff game. In a ruggedly fought encounter, the defense remained stout, but an ineffective offense resulted in an 8–3 loss.

The 1951 season began dismally. The team's number one draft pick, SMU All-American running back Kyle Rote, was sidelined for most of the year from a preseason injury and saw only spot duty. Conerly played the entire season with a shoulder injury that hampered his throwing. But the players hung tough, as workhorse running back Eddie Price established a league record of 271 carries and a team mark of 971 yards. The two losses to the Browns were costly, and the Giants found themselves in second place at season's end with a 9–2–1 record. "If we could only have beaten the goldarn Browns, we could have been the champs of everything," lamented Owen.

The Giants inaugurated the 1952 season with a run of three straight wins that included a defeat of the Browns. They were optimistic with a healthy Rote and a promising number one draft choice, All-American running back Frank Gifford of USC. Yet it was a strange year. The Giants beat Cleveland a second time but only had a 7–5 record to show for it. Amazingly, Tunnell produced more yardage on interceptions and kick returns (924) than the league's leading rusher.

It got worse in 1953. Rote and Price were out most of the season with injuries, which made Owen switch the highly talented Gifford to offense. Nothing helped. The Giants skidded to 3–9, their worst year since 1947. They were embarrassed at the end by absorbing a 62–14 hammering by the Browns. That was all Mara could take. After 23 years on the sidelines, Owen was released. It was the first time the Giants fired a coach, as the Giants always looked upon their team as a family.

Jim Lee Howell became the head coach when the 1954 season arrived. Before it did, Howell made a shrewd move by hiring Vince Lombardi, an assistant coach at Army. Howell also did all he could to prevent Conerly from retiring. Aching from the battering he absorbed the past two seasons, Conerly had had enough. Only after Howell promised him he would strengthen the offensive line did Conerly relent and agree to return. He enjoyed a good season, too, as did Gifford, who averaged a robust 5.6 yards a run as Howell's new-look Giants overcame 1953 with a 7–5 achievement.

Management looked north to the Canadian Football League in 1955 and set its sights on running back Alex Webster, the circuit's top rusher and MVP. Besides Webster, the Giants brought in defensive tackle Rosey Grier, defensive back Jimmy Patton, linebacker Harland Svare, and fullback Mel Triplett. "We are a strong team!" exclaimed Jack Mara. It didn't appear that way after the Giants lost their first three games. However, they managed to gel during the last five weeks of the season with four wins and a tie to salvage a 6–5–1 record.

Before the 1956 season started, the Giants were bolstering their defense as they left the Polo Grounds for Yankee Stadium. In trades, they got defensive end Andy Robustelli and defensive back Ed Hughes from the Rams. They also had an ample draft by getting center linebacker Sam Huff from West Virginia, defensive end Jim Katcavage from Dayton, and kicker Don Chandler from Florida. On paper, the Giants were loaded. They demonstrated it by winning six of their first seven games and went on to win the East with an 8–3–1 record, highlighted by Gifford's 819 rushing yards, a healthy average of 5.2 yards a carry, along with 51 receptions for 603 more yards.

On an extremely cold day in New York, the Giants faced the Bears, and they couldn't have played a better championship game. They powered a 34–7 halftime bulge on the way to a 47–7 rout. They prepared for it by remembering the 1934 "Sneakers Game." This time, it was a lot easier. They had Robustelli bring in four dozen sneakers from his sporting goods store in Connecticut.

Unfortunately, the championship bluster didn't carry over into 1957. The Giants appeared in control at 7–2 but floundered in the final three weeks by losing every game. What was painful was that two of the games were at home. Conerly, Gifford, and Chandler all had good years, but it wasn't enough. Still, the Giants had the foundation from the 1956 championship that would make them a force in the years ahead.

It would all maturate on a Sunday in December in 1958.

THE COLTS

Orphans Nobody Wanted

Before Johnny Unitas came along, Baltimore hadn't won a championship in any sport. The city was looked upon as a whistle stop between Washington, D.C., and New York on the Pennsylvania Railroad or the midpoint for motorists making their way north or south on I-95. Babe Ruth was born in Baltimore, but he didn't achieve his fame wearing anything with the name Baltimore attached to his uniform. Until the Babe's prodigious impact on the baseball world with the New York Yankees, Baltimore's most famous personality was easily perhaps Blaze Starr, a hot stripper, maybe the intellectual author H. L. Mencken, or possibly Edgar Allan Poe of another century for the minority of townsfolk who possessed literary affection. Blaze Starr and her leggy number shaking it downtown was where the action was, and she had quite a following of adoring fans. That is, until Unitas came along.

Yet the city did have its share of history, none more indelible than in the war of 1812. Francis Scott Key was so emotionally absorbed by the Americans repelling the mighty British army from capturing Baltimore that he wrote "The Star-Spangled Banner" while observing the flaming night action from Fort McHenry. The city never impressed Billy Martin, the acerbic New York Yankee manager.

"Baltimore is such a lousy town that Francis Scott Key went out in a boat to write 'The Star-Spangled Banner,'" snapped the feisty Martin.

Since Baltimore was one of the country's largest seaports, the Baltimore & Ohio railroad became a vital link for midwestern cities to ship their products for overseas delivery. In fact, the venerable B&O became the first railroad to introduce passenger travel. As the years progressed, Pimlico racetrack became famous as part of thoroughbred racing's Triple Crown in the spring, while Johns Hopkins facing Navy in lacrosse in the fall was arguably one of the city's biggest sports spectacles.

In 1950 Baltimore was in danger of living too completely in the past and needed change. It came in the form of a big urban renewal development known as the Charles Center. It occupied thirty-three acres of downtown, fully abundant with office buildings, apartments, a hotel, a theater, and a large department store. When the baseball Orioles appeared in 1954, the town realized a sports awakening. Oriole pride went all the way back to 1729, as the new birds took their colors of black and orange from the original colors of the Baltimore family that founded the city. The ebullience was pronounced in the harbor area, and nearby a Little Italy neighborhood attracted a steady stream of tourists.

Still, the doughty residents needed something to cheer for, someone, anyone, to embrace. That one person would turn out to be Unitas. He was the messenger who could deliver pride and respect to Baltimore. And the city needed both. Ruth, who was born in Baltimore, had left and never came back. He became the paragon with the Yankees in New York and bigger than life there. But that was the past. The future would be Unitas.

In reality, the Colts were portrayed as orphans in a town that was somehow symbolically linked to birds. Baltimore's first professional baseball team was called the Bluejays at home and, for some reason, the Orioles on the road. And Edgar Allan Poe wrote about a bird in his venerable classic, "The Raven." Then, in 1947, Baltimore inherited a bankrupt team from Miami called the Seahawks from the All-America Football Conference. Yet when the transplanted Miami team took up residence in Baltimore, they needed a new name. But what? A fan contest was held, and the winning entry became the newly named Colts. All the bird stories were put to rest.

A bizarre moment, one of several that would occur during the year, took place during an exhibition game. Baltimore trainer Fitz Lutz ran on the field to attend to center Mike Phillips, who was knocked unconscious from a severe blow. Lutz pulled back Phillips's eyelid and shockingly yelled out, "Ref, this man is dead!" One of Phillips's teammates restored calm. He explained to Lutz that Phillips had only one eye. Unfortunately, Lutz happened to pick the wrong one.

⬬

No professional team got off to a more paradoxical beginning than the frisky Colts in their silver-and-green jerseys under Coach Cecil Isbell, who had been a star with the Green Bay Packers. The historical occasion was on September 7 in a game against the Brooklyn Dodgers. An encouraging sign of the city's fan support was represented by 27,418 diehards, who sat in the rain at Municipal Stadium to witness the historic moment. They were dramatically rewarded on the opening kickoff.

The Dodgers' Elmore Harris, a track star who was positioned as a kick return specialist, had taken the kickoff 20 yards before he was stopped on the 25-yard line. He was hit so hard by Hub Bechtol that he fumbled. Harry Buffington, a Brooklyn lineman, scooped up the ball and made it to midfield, where he was hit and spun around. Despite the severity of the contact, he managed to hold on to the ball although dazed to some degree by the impact. Both end zones were equally far, and he chose one. Unfortunately for the visitors, it was the wrong one.

The gleeful Colts followed Buffington as he rumbled down-field in anticipation of a touchdown. As he approached the goal line, he regained his senses. He realized where he was and unloaded the ball behind him. Baltimore's Jim Castiglia caught it and hauntingly ran across the goal line. He was recorded in the maiden history book as the player who scored the Colts' first touchdown. They got another when halfback Billy Hillen-brand ran back the second-half kickoff 96 yards to propel Baltimore to a 16–7 victory.

Whatever euphoria Colts fans had that wet afternoon remained on the soggy field and with it the hope of a successful season. Baltimore lost its next eleven games before beating the Chicago Rockets, 14–7. They finished with an ignominious 2–11–1 record but were embraced as lovable losers by an adoring public. In a contest against the New York Yankees the last Sunday in September, 51,583 showed up and watched the Colts lose their third straight game, 21–7.

A 28–28 tie with San Francisco the following Sunday had 29,556 watching. But the Colts returned to their losing ways the very next week in Buffalo. The 20–15 loss generated sympathy nonetheless. The Colts appeared to have the winning touchdown on the last play of the game. Quarterback Bud Schwenk completed a long pass to Racehorse Davis, but the official claimed he stepped out of bounds on the 2-yard line before reaching the end zone.

The entire Colts bench stormed the field in a fervent protest. In a near riot, fights broke out among the fans and some of the players. When calm was finally achieved, the Colts players returned to their bench, only to discover that their blankets had been stolen. A compassionate 36,852 were in the stands as the Colts were routed by the Los Angeles Dons, 38–10, following the Buffalo game, while 20,574 showed up at the final game of the season and sat through a 42–0 debacle to the Cleveland Browns.

The fierce loyalty of the Baltimore faithful was apparent throughout the entire season. When the team would return from an away game, large crowds met them at the railroad station, and when they played those games along the eastern seaboard, special trains transported Colts fans to the games. One significant occasion was when the Colts played the Dodgers a second time. Some 2,000 diehards invaded Brooklyn accompanied by the fans' marching band. The team couldn't afford to transport the music makers, but the sixty-five members paid their own way.

Schwenk was Baltimore's first hero. He established a new passing record with 168 completions, which was 22 more than Isbell's mark at Green Bay. Two others did, too. Washington's Sammy Baugh (210) and Chicago's Sid Luckman (176) were tops, but Schwenk was in good company. The Colts averaged an attractive 28,000 fans for their home games, but, unfortunately, it wasn't enough economically. The cost of operating against the established National Football League and the Canadian Football League was too costly. The first of future Colts crises surfaced when ownership decided to pull out. The unexpected move created a dark cloud over the establishment of pro football in Baltimore.

That was not lost on Mayor Thomas D'Alessandro, who years later would play a key role in bringing major league baseball to the city. He called a number of civic and business leaders and nurtured a plan that would have seventeen of them each put up $20,000. Some 200 stockholders joined the group and contributed a solid financial foundation to operate and compete for players. Optimism prevailed when training camp convened.

However, once the 1948 preseason campaign began, it quickly dissipated. Overwhelming West Coast losses to Los Angeles and San Francisco left the owners distressed. Their fears were alleviated to some degree when the Colts defeated the Browns, 21–17, in Toledo behind the accurate passing of rookie quarterback Y. A. Tittle.

In the regular season opener against the Yankees, twenty-one-year-old Yelverton Abraham Tittle became an overnight hero. He threw for 346 yards, a league record, and added another by being involved in five touchdowns, one a handoff to Hillenbrand, in a feel-good 45–28 upset. The victory was an elixir as the Colts won three of their first four games, which left the city ecstatic. Every game became big now as the Colts remained in the Eastern Division race. It came down to the final game of the year against Buffalo, a team they had never beaten. Baltimore earned revenge from last year's meeting with a comforting 35–15 triumph. Some overenthusiastic fans compared the upset to Harry Truman's defeat of Thomas Dewey for the presidency a month earlier.

Baltimore and Buffalo were now deadlocked for the divisional championship with 7–7 records. A playoff game was scheduled the very next week, and Colts fans had the luxury of watching a second home game, the biggest one yet. However, in the days preceding the event, players and management were locked in a squabble over money. The players felt they should be given an extra half-game pay for the additional game. The rancor became so inflammatory that a strike was threatened. The players lost the dispute and appeared to have released their frustrations against the Bills.

They jumped into a 17–7 lead and appeared in control of the final outcome. The Bills remained calm and methodically pulled to within 3 points, 17–14, late in the fourth quarter. They were on their 40-yard line and moving to position a game-tying field goal. Quarterback George Ratterman tossed a short pass to halfback Chet Mutryn. He took three steps and fumbled. Baltimore tackle Johnny Mellus recovered the ball and had an unencumbered path to the end zone for the clinching touchdown. However, he was rebuked by an official's ruling of an incomplete pass to the chagrin of Colts fans and the disappointment of the coaches and players.

Ratterman made extraordinary use of a generous opportunity. Six plays later he completed a pass to the end zone to end Alton Baldwin for the winning touchdown as irate Colts fans descended with venomous fury on the field in pursuit of head linesman Tom Whelan, who made the highly inaccurate ruling on the pass. He had the good fortune of being rescued by players of both teams; otherwise he would have been inflicted with greater harm than a black eye and a torn shirt. Extra police were summoned, not only to quell the outbreak, but to disperse disgruntled fans who had set fire to a section of the wooden seats. It was an ugly sight and an unhappy conclusion to a successful season, one that demonstrated how passionate Baltimore fans were about their Colts. They moaned over the fact the Colts had twenty-four first downs to Buffalo's eleven and outgained them, 394 yards to 297.

◦

It came as no great revelation that Baltimore fans were expecting better Sundays in 1949. They had averaged over 29,000 people for eight home games, better than some other teams. It's just that management couldn't give them anything more, namely, players. Even after losing their first four games, fan support never wavered. Over 200 fans greeted them at the airport when they returned from a loss in Chicago. Yet the club's board of directors wasn't so ambiguous. They fired Isbell and named Walter Driskill, the team's president and general manager, to replace him. Ironically, Driskill had voted against firing Isbell.

"I didn't seek this job, and now that I've got it, I don't want it," he declared to the players. "I got out of coaching two years ago, and I didn't want to get back in. I have gotten to know Cecil Isbell well in the past two years. I've grown fond of him, and I can't say I'm enjoying this situation. But we've got a game with Cleveland Sunday, and we'd better get to work."

It didn't help. They lost their last six games and finished 1–11, but the fans remained faithful. After a season-ending 38–14 rout in Buffalo, over 5,000 persons waited for them at the airport. Weeks later, the AAFC and the NFL ended their four-year war. Cleveland, San Francisco, and Baltimore were absorbed into the older league. Yet another crisis surfaced. The team had lost money, and the group that operated in the past two years refused to invest any more despite being incorporated into the NFL.

George Preston Marshall, the baronial owner of the Redskins 40 miles to the south who always considered Baltimore part of his domain, kept a keen eye on the Colts' dilemma. He relished the thought that indeed the franchise would fold after three years of financial losses.

The new owner of the Colts was Abraham Watner, who didn't know anything about football. He was a guy who owned a cemetery, and before the 1950 season ended, he literally buried the team. It didn't cost him any moving expenses either. He operated the Colts from his cemetery office. An associate who worked closely with Watner tried to understand why Watner had any business getting into pro football in the first place.

"Abe got interested in pro football through Marshall, who always made money in Washington," he explained. "He wanted a pro football team as a plaything, and I don't think he would have minded losing a little money. But after he got in, he began to realize that a man could drop a quarter of a million right quick, and he lost his nerve. Once that dawned on him, everything he did from then on was with one idea in mind, to cut his eventual losses to the bone."

Watner went about it in a capricious way even before the season began. At training camp, he felt the trainers were using an excessive amount of adhesive tape and almost came to blows with head trainer Mickey McLernon when he ordered him to use less. Watner also decided that too much chewing gum was being dispersed and wanted each player to receive only a half-stick before the start of every practice. The atmosphere at camp became confusing with each passing day.

A scouting report labeled Arthur Bok of Dayton University as a great defensive prospect. Less than a week into camp, Bok told new coach Clem Crowe that he was confused and wanted to return home. Later it was learned that Bok never played defense at Dayton. The comical cemetery Colts were further laughed at when it was learned that due to an injury, Bok never played in the game on which the scout reported.

One morning Crowe joined the huddle with his players. He was overcome by a smell of alcohol and looked straight at rookie center Joel Williams.

"My God," Crowe yelled. "Not so early in the morning."

"No, coach," replied Williams. "That's from last night." Williams never made the team.

The comedic environment continued in the exhibition season in San Antonio, where the Colts would play the Los Angeles Rams. Clark Shaughnessy was fired as the Rams coach weeks earlier and replaced by Joe Stydahar. He met with Crowe, determined to fulfill an earlier boast that "when Stydahar gets through with this team, I can take a high school team and beat them. Try to score on them early, and the Rams will fall apart." Well, the Colts must have been a grade school team that night in a 70–21 mauling.

When the season opened, the players were traumatized. They lost their first six games and their last five, at least showing consistency, and finished 1–11. They set a new record for points allowed in twelve games, being outscored 462–213. Some of the more one-sided results were 38–14 to Washington, 55–13 to the Chicago Cardinals, 70–27 to the Los Angeles Rams, 55–20 to the New York Giants, and 51–14 to the New York Yanks. Watner threw in the towel and sold the players to the league for the princely sum of $50,000. The tragicomedy ended with the Colts helmets winding up in Green Bay as the players were scattered around the league.

❧

George Preston Marshall looked at Baltimore with a jaundiced eye. He always felt that the Redskins had a Baltimore market before the Colts arrived and wanted it back. He didn't hesitate in making it known, either.

"We'll be known in the future as the Washington–Baltimore Redskins, and you can't buy the team for a million dollars," pronounced Marshall. "Maryland, and of course Baltimore, is an integral part of our Redskin setup. You can say for me that it will remain so as long as I am running the club. We will never relinquish the territory again."

Marshall's selfish remarks didn't play well in Baltimore. A number of members from the old board acted and hired a lawyer to institute a suit against the NFL, the premise being that Watner didn't have the right to sell the corporation's assets, principally its players, without the authorization of the stockholders, and that the league made an illegal purchase. On October 2, 1951, the suit was filed. All the directors wanted was the return of pro football to Baltimore.

There was hope from another source. If Ted Collins, the owner of the Yanks, decided to move his team out of New York, Baltimore, with its rabid fan base, would be the ideal city. Collins did call it quits after the 1951 season, but the league, probably with Marshall applying pressure, awarded the team to Dallas. The tenacious board members wouldn't quit. Led by Zanvyl Krieger, they kept after Commissioner Bert Bell after they received a favorable court ruling on June 6, 1952.

"Bert, we aren't trying to get you over a barrel," explained Krieger. "We just want a team back. Doggone it, Bert, we could sell 15,000 season tickets if we had a team back here."

Bell wasn't so sure.

"What makes you think so?" he challenged.

"I don't know," answered Krieger. "It's just a feeling I have. Twenty thousand is too high, and ten thousand would be too low. We've already sold that many in our best year. We can do it. I know we can."

At a December 3 meeting of the Advertising Club in Baltimore, Bell informed the members that the city would return to the league if it could meet one condition: that was to sell 15,000 season tickets in six weeks. With the Christmas holidays approaching, it was a mammoth challenge. But that was the number Krieger mentioned, and Bell put in play.

Bruce Livie, one of Maryland's largest automobile dealers, was named chairman of the ticket drive. Like Santa Claus, he delivered. He set up shop at Municipal Stadium and put his sales force in action. In just four weeks and three days, to be exact, Livie reached the goal, and Baltimore had a team again. Or did it?

Bell promised the Baltimore denizens a team, and he kept his word. It came in the form of the transplanted Texans from Dallas. This was the same franchise that flopped in Boston and became a ward of the league. It was almost as if Livie had a manifest for a used car. Bell also assured the group that he would provide a backer to finance the team, but he didn't have one at the moment. Now he was on the spot after the board's successful ticket drive that was made two weeks earlier than the prescribed time.

Determinedly, Bell reached back to his coaching years at the University of Pennsylvania in putting the team's financial hierarchy together. He arranged for Don Kellett, once a three-sport captain at Penn, to become the general manager and named Keith Molesworth as coach. Everyone was in place except the most important one, the owner. Bell continued with his Penn connection and approached Carroll Rosenbloom, a star running back, who played under Bell. Rosenbloom was now a wealthy textile manufacturer and a summer neighbor of Bell in the Jersey shore town of Margate.

The dapper Rosenbloom had a 600-acre estate on the Eastern Shore of Maryland and had decided it was time to live in luxury as a country squire. He would concern himself only with a gigantic peach orchard that presented an ample financial reward if he wanted to engage in the fruit business.

At first, Rosenbloom was reluctant, but Bell finally succeeding in convincing him to become a 52 percent owner who would be joined by Krieger and Livie. All they needed now were players, and that was Kellett's responsibility.

Some of the players returned to Baltimore, while others had retired, and still others went to Canada. Art Donovan, a rough-and-tough defensive tackle who saw action with the Marines in the Pacific and played only one season with Baltimore, decided to stay after his experience in Dallas.

"We had no talent to begin with," acknowledged Donovan. "We played just four games, but it didn't pay. The few fans who did bother to come out and watch us treated us nice enough, but high school and college football were still the draw in Texas. Every Monday morning when we were paid, Coach Jimmy Phelan would stand there next to the paymaster's window and say, 'Now, don't hesitate, boys; get right on down to the bank and cash that sucker.'

"When the season ended, I drove my car back from Dallas, and on the drive home to New York I stopped in Baltimore to renew some old acquaintances. There was something special about the town for me. I had the feeling even then that was where I'd end up spending the rest of my life."

The Colts marching band returned in full force as the new Colts prepared for the 1953 season. The band dispersed in the two years of the team's absence. Colts fans' interest was then directed at the 49ers. There were two prominent reasons for it. San Francisco was a member of the vanquished AAFC, and on a personal note, Y. A. Tittle had gone there when the old Colts folded. It was strange that Baltimore, an eastern city, found itself in the NFL's Western Division, of all places. Colts fans didn't care. They had their team back.

There were a lot of new faces on the roster, mainly from the defunct Texans, namely, Donovan, Gino Marchetti, Buddy Young, George Taliaferro, Tom Keane, Joe Campanella, Brad Ecklund, Ken Jackson, Barney Poole, and Sisto Averno. They traded for veterans like Art Spinney, Carl Taseff, and Don Shula while signing rookies Bill Pellington and Tom Finnin. It didn't matter if Mickey Mouse were in a Colts uniform. They would have cheered him, too.

The regular season opened at home against the Chicago Bears, and Colts fans, 23,715 of them, cheered a 13–9 victory over the favored Bears through the heroics of rugged defensive back Bert Rechichar. He was blind in one eye, but there wasn't anyone tougher, and he looked the part. Rechichar ran 6 yards with an intercepted pass and later brought the crowd to its feet with a booming record 56-yard field goal.

Yet it was a defeat in the fourth game of the season that convinced Rosenbloom he was in football to stay. The 2–1 Colts were playing the winless Packers in Green Bay. However, they were shockingly upended, 37–14. One particular play made a concrete impression on the owner. In the closing minutes, with the Colts hopelessly beaten, Taliaferro ran back a punt for good yardage along the sideline while being chased by a couple of Packers. Instead of stepping out of bounds, he put his head down and picked up an additional 2 yards.

"If they play that hard, I want to go with them all the way," exclaimed Rosenbloom. "If they've got that kind of spirit, I can't sit back, can I?"

When the team returned from Green Bay, some 4,000 fans greeted them at the airport. The very next Sunday, the players showed their appreciation by defeating the hated Redskins, 27–17, making Marshall eat his demeaning words that "the Colts were a bunch of castoffs." Sorrowfully, that was Baltimore's final win of the year. They lost their next seven games and finished 3–9. Still, the Colts had their best season financially, the first time the club had ever finished out of the red. It made an impact on Rosenbloom. A week or so before Christmas, the benevolent Rosenbloom gave forty players and coaches each a $500 bonus and even threw the team a party.

"Baltimore deserves a winner," proclaimed the suave owner. "I am promising you that winner. I don't care how much money it takes, because from now until we get a winner, I won't be giving the proper time to my own business."

How could anyone not like Rosenbloom? He made a promise to the public, and in five years he would deliver and become one of the league's power brokers.

The Colts' faithful proved their loyalty in 1954, as 30,000 of them purchased season tickets, the largest amount ever. Rosenbloom was thrilled and determined more than ever to make the Colts winners. He reasoned that he couldn't get Paul Brown, the best in the business, and opted instead for one of his assistants, Weeb Ewbank. He moved Coach Keith Molesworth into the front office as director of scouting to procure better players. He made an impact in the college draft by selecting Ordell Braase, Alex Sandusky, and Raymond Berry and signed an undrafted Buzz Nutter.

An ex-boxer, Elmer Willhoite, had Ewbank wondering what he had gotten himself into. He was obtained in a trade with the Browns and didn't even know the names of all the teams in the league. But what made Ewbank wonder all the more was Willhoite's warm-up exercises during an exhibition game in Pittsburgh. He went under the goal posts and started hitting them with his shoulders. Fans looked on in amazement as the posts were swaying from side to side. Apparently, Willhoite punched himself out along the way and never played a regular season game.

Winning four of five exhibition games had Colts fans a bit giddy. It was an aberration. The Colts were successful only one time in their first nine outings that was blemished by a seven-game losing streak on the way to a 3–9 campaign. The opening game home loss to the Rams, 48–0, was an embarrassment in Ewbank's coaching debut. It was a young squad, one that had only nineteen of its original thirty-nine players from the 1953 team. Ewbank was a stickler on detail and discipline. On away games, the players experienced Ewbank's pronouncement to regimentation. He would hand the hotel's food manager a menu, of which Donovan kept a copy:

Please place at separate tables the various orders to facilitate service by waiters. It has been found in the past that

things run smoother if the tables are labeled with cards list-
ing the food to be served and the names of the men to be
served at that table.

Please serve beef bouillon to all persons eating the pre-
game meal. Also, French, Roquefort, and Russian dressing
are to be available on each table, along with toast, butter,
honey, and pitchers of coffee. No milk is to be served at the
pregame meal.

No one is to be served the lettuce salad or the baked
potato, since a number of the boys do not want either.
Therefore, place on a separate table fifteen baked potatoes
and thirty lettuce salads—and those persons who desire
either may help themselves.

Please place the steaks (and other orders) on the
respective tables, promptly at 9:00 a.m., making sure that
the well-done meat is really well done and will not have to
be returned to the kitchen for additional cooking.

If it is necessary for you to hire more help to get the
meal out on time, then please do so. Thank you. Weeb
Ewbank.

"We finished 3–9 again, but it was a good 3–9, if you know
what I mean," believed Donovan, who made the Pro Bowl.

Baltimore acquired a significant amount of talent in the 1955
draft. It began with the team's bonus pick, Oregon's George
Shaw, the most sought after quarterback in the country. They
followed that with number one pick fullback Alan Ameche of
Wisconsin, center Dick Szymanski of Notre Dame, running
back, L. G. Dupre of Baylor, guard Jack Patera of Oregon and
guard George Preas of VPI. All would become starters. Berry,
who was drafted in 1954, reported to training camp with the

rookies. He, too, made the starting lineup after having remained at SMU to play his final season of college ball.

Berry made an immediate impression with his off-field regimen. Nobody had ever seen anything like it before. It began at training camp, where he would wash his own practice pants because he liked the way they fit. He didn't want a different pair from one day to the next and to have to adjust accordingly. At breakfast, he wanted to have his eggs done in a certain way and did so by cooking them himself. Quite often on the road games, Berry would walk around the lobby of the hotel with a football tucked under his arms, fingering it on occasion. He felt that when the game began, he would have a better feel for the ball.

In the season-opening game against the Bears, Ameche made a vivid imprint that even he couldn't have imagined. He was warming up before the kickoff with Shaw, two rookies trying to shake the jitters.

"Hey, Horse, what are you and I doing out here?" yelled Shaw.

"I wish somebody would tell me," shrugged Ameche.

On the first play of the game, Shaw handed off the ball to the big fullback, and he knew what to do. He broke loose like a wild stallion for a 79-yard touchdown.

The Colts busted out of the corral the first three weeks by not losing a game.

Before the opening game win over the Bears, the players were told about Campanella's mother, who was seriously ill in a Cleveland hospital. Her heart did stop beating, but she was miraculously revived by the doctors. All the players knelt in prayer and dedicated the game to her. Campanella's mother regained her health, and the thankful bunch of players promised one another that the entire season would be played in honor of all their mothers.

However, they couldn't maintain their gallop, and after eight games they stood 4–4. Baltimore lost its final two games to finish

5-6-1. If it was any consolation, they did manage to improve upon the 1954 season, yet it didn't sit well with Rosenbloom. He held Ewbank responsible for the collapse and looked in the direction of Buddy Parker, who was fired by Detroit. But Pittsburgh signed him before Rosenbloom could even make an offer.

When Baltimore made Penn State's Lenny Moore their first choice in the 1956 draft, the Colts had a genuine breakaway runner they had lacked. Yet it was the signing of a little known sandlot quarterback that would make the biggest impact. Almost overnight he would expound everyone's imagination and the fortunes of the woebegone Colts for the next decade. It was Johnny Unitas. No one expected Unitas to play that season. Shaw was considered one of the top quarterbacks in the league and had an excellent opening game win against the Bears, completing nineteen of twenty-five passes for 231 yards and two touchdowns in the 28-21 win. However, three weeks later against the Bears in Chicago, Shaw incurred a season-ending leg injury.

A nervous Unitas was rushed into action and fumbled twice and had two interceptions in his first four series. He looked every bit a sandlotter. After the game, management pushed the panic button. They extended a help call to Gary Kerkorian, who had left the team before the season to pursue a law degree at Georgetown. He was needed. After the Chicago debacle, Unitas settled down, went 4-4, and exhibited promise as the Colts finished 5-7. Kellett pointed to the 38-33 loss to Green Bay in Milwaukee the third game of the year as the divider of a winning season.

"That was the key to our entire season," lamented Kellett.

If anything, Ewbank enjoyed a deep, personal satisfaction in the 21-7 victory over the Browns. It was a game that he wanted to win more than any other. It was the Colts first win over Cleveland in the team's history after seven previous defeats. In the loss, the Browns were eliminated from title contention for the first time since 1946, their first year of operation. After the game, Paul Brown ran past Ewbank and ignored him by not shaking his hand.

In 1957 the Colts got two players in the draft who would ultimately forge a championship team. Their first pick was tackle Jim Parker of Ohio State, followed by linebacker Don Shinnick of UCLA. With pressure mounting, Ewbank tightened the everyday regimen at training camp.

"I like this squad," gushed Rosenbloom. "It's the best I've seen in early training, but it should be. We think we're good, but remember there are eleven other teams in eleven other camps that feel the same way."

There were whispers that this could be Ewbank's last season as Baltimore opened the campaign with a vengeance from the defense in humbling Detroit, 34–14. Marchetti appeared in the Lions backfield practically all afternoon. One time he sacked Bobby Layne and almost ripped the quarterback's jersey off his back. Layne got up in disgust and slammed the football to the ground. When Tobin Rote relieved the battered Layne, he was subjected to the same pressure.

The physicality of the Colts line condensed Detroit's running game to 23 yards. Unitas took care of the offense with four touchdown passes in a convincing performance. The win was costly, as Pellington was sidelined for the year with a fractured arm. Despite the overwhelming win, Paul Menton of the *Baltimore Evening Sun* issued a cautionary thought:

From one game at least, it is difficult to imagine a better looking team than the Colts. The problem will be to maintain that kind of sharpness over 11 more weeks. Few teams ever have.

They were equally effective against the Bears the following week, as 6,000 more fans swelled the turnstile count to 46,558 in Municipal Stadium. The theatrics shone in the second half as the Colts overcame a 10–7 halftime deficiency in producing a 21–10 win. Shinnick, who replaced Pellington, led a defense that squeezed the powerful Bears ground attack to 29 yards. Unitas delivered the victory with two fourth-quarter touchdown passes. Ewbank claimed that the daring play selection was all Unitas' doing.

"Let's play them one at a time," warned Ewbank when talk began circulating about a championship.

The Colts had Baltimore celebrating following a third successive win against Green Bay, 45–17. The Packers runners also were stifled, gaining only 42 yards as the Colts secondary intercepted five passes. Baltimore overcame a 10–7 halftime shortfall and scored 38 points in the final two quarters. Was it any wonder that some 5,000 supporters greeted them at the airport?

They certainly were playing like champions, but could they maintain that caliber of play? The answer came suddenly and unforeseen. A fool's paradise was exposed in the next three weeks beginning with the Lions in Detroit. Two Unitas touchdown passes had the Colts serenely ahead, 27–3. In the third period the Lions roared from their slumber by recovering three fumbles in the final three minutes to engender a startling 31–27 upset. It was a dazed and silent group of players on the plane back to Baltimore.

The next night at a dinner, Rosenbloom still felt confident about the rest of the season. He was positive in his remarks as he addressed the audience.

"We're a great team," he began. "When we won three straight, there was enough glory to go all around. Now that we have lost a game, we will all absorb the blame. No coach or player lost the Detroit game. We all lost it."

Yet, against the Packers six days after Rosenbloom's encouraging remarks, the Colts allowed another game to dissipate in the final minute, twenty-nine seconds from the whistle. The 24–21 loss left 48,510 patrons heartbroken since a Unitas touchdown aerial with just over a minute left had given Baltimore an apparent 21–17 victory. The downward spiral continued a week later at home against Pittsburgh in a 19–13 upset. The alarming conclusion was that the Colts played poorly as they fell to 3–3 and could have easily been 6–0. Criticism was directed at Ewbank.

"I know football, and I know what I am doing is right," he testily answered back. "We are still building, and I feel I'm doing my job. But if I don't have this one, I'll have another one in football," was his parting shot.

Ewbank had to rally his players, and he did. The Colts kicked back and won four consecutive games, the longest winning streak in their history. The good fortune advanced their record to 7–3, one game lead over Detroit and San Francisco. The seven wins assured them of having their first winning season. They had two road games left and needed just a tie for the division title and advancement to a playoff game.

However, the away games were in California, which had been a tombstone over the years for the Colts. They had won only once in the badlands, in 1954, against a dissension-racked Ram team, 22–11.

The first stop was San Francisco, where Tony Bennett's city by the bay was seized with delirium. Police on horseback were summoned to quell a riot when an estimated 5,000 fans mulled around Kezar Stadium looking to purchase end zone seats that were placed on sale the morning of the game. It was a hot ticket. Scalpers were asking and getting $100 for a ticket. Fans had camped out overnight to assure themselves of getting the best opportunity at the remaining seats. When most of them couldn't, they began rocking the wooden ticket booths and almost tore down the iron accordion gates. The wild scene left an impression on Cameron Snyder of the *Baltimore Evening Sun*. He wrote: "It was the kind of excitement which gripped an entire city. And it's doubtful if anything, short of an earthquake, ever hit San Francisco with the impact of the Colts–49ers game."

The Colts were a confident bunch. Two weeks earlier they had defeated San Francisco, 27–21, and followed that with a 31–14 win over Los Angeles. Their chances of winning one of the two games were better than average. Baltimore dominated the first-half action, but several costly mistakes contributed to a 3-point deficit. The 49ers scored first on a Colts interference penalty. A Unitas-to-Moore throw that accumulated 47 yards to the 49er 12-yard line was wasted by Moore's fumble. The speedy halfback did manage to make up for his miscue by scampering for 82 yards with a Unitas pass and a 13–9 second-half lead. The Colts failed to extend their advantage by blowing two field goal attempts.

Still, Baltimore was in control with the scoreboard clock indicating two minutes left in the tense struggle. Onetime Colts hero Y. A. Tittle brought the 49ers back with a 30-yard pass to Hugh McElhenny that reached the Colts 15-yard line. Baltimore's defense stopped the next two plays, and when Tittle got hurt and had to leave the game, the Colts were close to a win. Rookie John Brodie replaced Tittle and threw a desperate wobbly pass into the end zone. McElhenny got behind a Colts defender and made a leaping catch for the touchdown that buried Baltimore, 17–13.

The Colts remained on the West Coast, where Ewbank had to regroup his dejected players for the Rams game. They desperately needed a victory but didn't come close. Norm Van

Brocklin, one of the NFL's top quarterbacks, made sure of it. He had a premium day, throwing for four touchdowns in a smashing 37–21 victory that sent the Colts home as losers with a 7–5 record. Rosenbloom wept openly and unabashedly in his press box seat.

It didn't matter that Unitas came away with the Jim Thorpe Trophy as the player of the year with a league best twenty-four touchdown passes. Unitas would rather have the championship. They just couldn't overcome the West Coast jinx.

On the long, solemn flight back to Baltimore, Ewbank was left worrying whether he would coach again in 1958.

GIANTS  1958 SEASON

Tenacity

By the time the Giants reported to training camp for the 1958 season, Elvis Presley had been drafted into the Army, Arnold Palmer had captured the Masters, Tim Tam had won the Kentucky Derby, and UCLA's Rafer Johnson had set a decathlon record of 8,302 points in Moscow. The Giants experienced a newsworthy event, at least for them. Instead of assembling at St. Michael's College in Winooski, Vermont, where they had been the last four years, Wellington Mara took Samuel Gompers's advice and headed west to Salem, Oregon, and Willamette University. He researched and found the oldest university in the West, which was founded in 1842, some thirty-four years after the Lewis and Clark expedition, to perhaps keep some of his fun-loving players from the proximity of New York and its lively night spots, especially Toots Shor's. The quantum move clearly signified that.

Wellington was passionate over what happened two years earlier only to be disappointed the very next year. In 1956 the Giants had moved into Yankee Stadium and won their first championship in eighteen years. They did so with a thunderous performance against the Chicago Bears, 47–7, the Giants' highest point total in nine championship playoffs. Wellington reasoned that the decisive victory would be the clarion for the rest of the decade. He had built a veteran team, made some shrewd trades for player talent, and blended the roster with some excellent draft choices. Mara felt strongly that his team would repeat in 1957. They were on the way to accomplishing it with an Eastern Division–leading 7–2 record only to stumble and lose the final three games, two of which were played in Yankee Stadium.

The 1956 championship was the hallmark of any in Giants history. It even attracted the attention of Commissioner Bert Bell, who compared it to the Bears 73–0 mauling of the Redskins in the 1940 championship contest. The Giants defense kept the Bears as docile as playful cubs, and the offense did the rest. New York's third title was practically won on the opening kickoff. Gene Filipski, a rookie running back, carried George Blanda's kick 53 yards to the Bears 39-yard line. Four plays later, Mel Triplett broke loose on a 17-yard touchdown run to warm the hearts of 58,836 who looked on in 20-degree weather. The attendance was 10,000 less than accepted because of the extreme cold.

Triplett's run was specifically designed by Assistant Coach Vince Lombardi. In studying game films, he detected that Chicago's two middle linemen pinched together as a precaution against a draw play. He also noted that the Bears often kept a middle guard behind both as added protection. Lombardi outlined the play for Triplett in which he would head up the middle and then cut either left or right and head for daylight.

The manner in which the Giants dominated the Bears the entire game shocked those in attendance as much as members of the press chronicling the game. With one notable exception, it was the 1934 game between the two teams all over again. The field was also frozen then when the Giants switched from the conventional cleats to sneakers in what came to be known as the "Sneakers Game." They overcame a 13–3 halftime shortfall to overtake Chicago for their first championship. This time, the Giants were well ahead at intermission, 34–7, which convinced a large number of the crowd to leave for the warmth of their homes.

Led by Andy Robustelli, the Giants defense held the Bears star running back, Rick Casares, to just 43 yards on thirteen carries. They also contained the celebrated Bears trio of quarterbacks George Blanda and Ed Brown and end Harlon Hill, who had six meaningless receptions. The Giants final two touchdowns in the second half were created by quarterback Charlie Conerly, who finished the game seven of ten for 195 yards that included a 67-yard pass play to Frank Gifford.

Jim Lee Howell, in his third year as coach, got the Giants a long-awaited crown. He prepared his team with only six practice sessions in the two weeks leading up to the game. Afterwards, he had high tribute for the thirty-two-year-old Conerly, who had his share of critics.

"I was particularly pleased to see Chuck play one of his finest games because so many people seemed to think we couldn't win with him," praised Howell. "He showed everybody what a poised, skilled pro he is in his biggest game. This is the closest thing to a perfect game that I had ever seen. I don't think any team could handle the Bears like that."

It was such a convincing victory that it even elicited raves from the Chicago players and coaches. They made no excuses for their ineptitude and simply credited the Giants.

"They hit us hard at the start, and they never stopped hitting hard," remarked Rick Casares. "Even in the last two minutes, when you think a team leading like that would ease up, they didn't. This is the toughest team I've ever faced."

There were no alibis from head coach Paddy Driscoll. He respected the Giants' effort that overwhelmed his team.

"The frozen field and their sneakers had nothing to do with it," he began. "We carry sneakers all the time. Our shoes were just as suitable as their sneakers. It was the same for both sides. There is nothing you can say after a defeat like this. The Giants played a great game."

The Giants celebrated well into the night at Toots Shor's, their favorite oasis. It was more than Conerly, Gifford, and Rote this time, the usual regulars, but a whole bunch of them. There were so many revelers that Toots had to block out the entire back of the joint to accommodate them. Rosey Brown, in a sonic moment, lifted Gifford off the floor and shouted, "We are champions." Everyone else picked it up from there and yelled the same thing. It was a golden night, and there were a few who observed the dawn.

Several hours before the game began, Howell did secure an edge regarding the footwear. He dispatched defensive back Ed Hughes and Gene Filipski onto the field. Hughes wore cleats and Filipski sneakers. Hughes ran a few steps, made his cuts, and slipped to the ground. Filipski did much the same thing but remained upright. That was enough for Howell. He ordered the entire team to wear sneakers.

A month earlier, the Giants had suffered a heartbreaking 17–17 tie against the Bears in Yankee Stadium. New York was enjoying what appeared to be a safe 17–0 lead as the second half started, but Hill led the Bears' comeback with two long touchdown receptions of 79 and 56 yards. The final one was a sensational acrobatic catch that defied the imagination. Covered by two defenders, Hill nevertheless managed to tip Brown's pass, first on the 5-yard line, again on the 3, and finally on the 2 before falling into the end zone and the game-tying touchdown with less than two minutes remaining. It was the final frustration of a game in which Casares, the league's leading rusher, only managed 13 yards on thirteen carries. The savage Giants defense held the entire Bears ground game to 12 net yards.

"We dominated the game and should have won," said Sam Huff. "They were lucky to tie us. Hill made the greatest catch. We had [Jimmy] Patton and [Dick] Nolan on him, and I'll be damned if he didn't make a circus catch. He couldn't have done it again if we didn't have anybody covering him. It was just one of those things. It was a Hail Mary pass that worked for them."

Huff strongly felt that the tie game with the Bears was the turning point in the future success of the franchise. It was the reason why Wellington Mara was dismayed by the late-season collapse in 1957. Beginning with the 1954 campaign, when Howell took over as coach, the Giants were an ensemble that produced four straight winning seasons after the 3–9 swoon in 1953, which was Steve Owen's final as head coach. The first two appointments Howell made were tantamount for his and the team's success. He made Tom Landry his defensive coach and made a solid hire in reaching out to West Point to bring in Vince Lombardi as offensive coach. The players readily accepted both.

Landry was in reality a player-coach in the defensive back-field his last two years as an active player. He had a profound knowledge of the game almost to the point of being a genius with his defensive scheme. He looked more like a college professor than a coach, spoke softly with a Texas twang, dressed conservatively, and made an immediate impact on the players he performed with for six years.

"Tom was an innovator who invented the four-three defense," gushed Kyle Rote, an offensive performer, no less. "He refined it. He established it. And I'll tell you something else he did. He started the idea of having separate meetings for the offense and defense. Under Steve Owen, we all met at the same time. In '54 we started winning again with our defense. And Tom decided to take his guys into another room. I think he figured that if the defense had to sit there while we drew up the game plan for the offense, they'd get discouraged.

"He did me a great favor. I used to run patterns against Tom in practice. When both my knees were shot, Tom talked Howell into moving me out to wide receiver. I couldn't really run out of the backfield anymore. I couldn't get out of the way of my own people."

Lombardi's persona was completely opposite Landry's. He was more emotional and demonstrative. His booming voice was his trademark. He was a great lineman in college, one of Fordham's "Seven Blocks of Granite," as the Rams offensive line was called. Howell actually hired Lombardi, who flew from New York to talk with him on his farm in Arkansas following a phone call from Wellington.

"The Maras were Fordham people and Catholics, and they recommended him," laughed Howell. "He had a great background. He was at West Point then, on Earl Blaik's staff. I knew him. He used to come out to our training camps.

"He flew down to Lonoke to see if we could stand each other. Some friends had dropped off some wild duck, and we fixed it for dinner. Vince seemed to like it, and we got along fine. The Maras didn't want to force him on me, but I said, sure, I knew he would help us.

"There was never any doubt where Lombardi was headed. Every time a job opened up, he asked me if I minded if he applied for it. The question you had about Landry was whether he was too smart to be a coach. He worked for an oil company in the off-season and had the brains to be a fine engineer. Both were brilliant; both had a lot of drive. Especially Vince."

In a convoluted way, the three were a strange mix of personalities, yet an embarrassment of riches: the head coach never wanted to be one and never sought the position, a defensive coach who was an engineer, and an offensive coach who was somewhat of a puzzle to those around him. Yet they all got along fine and created the family atmosphere the Maras always wanted.

It was Wellington who wanted Howell, who had been an end coach under Owen after his nine-year playing career with the Giants ended in 1948. After the 1953 season, Howell was preparing for his annual drive back to Arkansas when Wellington called and asked him to stop by the office. Howell tried to beg off, but Wellington insisted. Howell delayed his trip out of loyalty. He had known Mara since 1937, when he reported to the Giants as an end out of the University of Arkansas. Howell liked the family feeling the Maras created and nurtured a friendship with Wellington.

"As a kid, Wellington took the game films for us, was still doing it when I became coach. He had a Polaroid, and he'd sit in the press box and take still pictures when the other team went into a formation we hadn't seen. Then he'd put the snapshots in a wool football sock with a weight inside and swing it down to the bench.

"I didn't want to coach, really, not at all. But I liked football and thought that I had something to offer. I just wanted to coach a couple of years to see how it was. I wasn't cut out to coach, frankly. You have to kick people around, and I didn't like that. Never did."

By 1958 the Giants defense was acknowledged as the best in the league. New Yorkers passionately embraced them, and Giants fans were the first to echo "Dee-Fense" when they appeared on the field in a critical situation. It was a tribute to Landry and his guile, and the fan adulation wasn't lost on Madison Avenue, where the advertising moguls began to use some of the players, notably Huff, as marketing personalities. More than any other player, Huff symbolized the Giants' thorny defense.

"Landry charted every play the opponents had," disclosed Huff. "He had their tendencies down pat, and he signaled us from the sideline on how to set up. We had what we called the four-three key, inside or outside. When it was inside, our two tackles would shut down the middle, and I would go with the flow of the backs.

"On the outside four-three key, the tackles would go out, and I would go inside. Everybody had to be able to tackle. From my point of view, one exceptional thing about Landry's defense was that it was so coordinated that I was rarely blocked."

Huff made it sound easy. It was much more intricate than that. Whoever had the responsibility of calling the defensive signals in the huddle would blurt out a girl's name. When he wanted to refer to Harland Svare, he called him Wanda. Sam Huff was Meg, and Howie Livingston was Sara. The defensive codes were not limited to female names. The fun began when they lined up against the offense. Then a list of colors—red, yellow, blue, and green—was called to further confuse an opponent. The secondary had its own verbiage to implement different types of pass defense. Dance names like mambo or tango were used.

"Girls' names are nice," said Huff. "They sort of draw the tension away in the huddle."

Landry was very positive in his theory of defense, an absolute student of the game. He would explain his doctrine simply yet effectively. He was so meticulous that none of the players would question him. That alone spelled volumes.

"I remember once when Tom was explaining a defensive setup," said Howell. "Now, every defense has a weakness if you can spot it. One of our players pointed out the weakness Tom had just described. He asked what would happen if the offense did a certain thing.

"'They won't do it,' remarked Landry. 'But what if they did?' challenged the player. 'They won't do it, so don't worry about it,' Tom repeated. Tom was right. They didn't do it."

Howell, a hands-off coach, gave both Landry and Lombardi an open forum. He let each determine strategy. Down deep

Howell felt that, indeed, he did have two genius minds that he could depend on and never worry about preparedness from either one.

"I can remember walking down our dormitory in training camp in St. Michael's," said Rote. "I'd look up to the left and see Lombardi running his plays. Then on down the hall, I'd look in Howell's room and see him reading the newspaper.

"We lost our first three preseason games in 1957, and Vince decided he had to do something drastic. So he threw a beer party, which was way out of character. I think Vince wanted to show us that he wasn't always the tough S.O.B. he seemed to be. Everybody drank as much beer as they could handle. The next day at practice it was really a comedy. Guys were trying to field punts, and the ball would hit them on the helmet.

"I wouldn't say Lombardi was a Napoleon type. But he was this barrel-chested guy that demanded your attention. He would chalk plays on the blackboard, and his voice would boom throughout the room. You believed him then if you hadn't before.

"Landry attacked things in a different way, low-keyed and very serious. But he could intimidate you mentally the same way Lombardi did physically. Tom got away with it because he was always right."

Howell made it work. He was an easygoing southerner almost to the point of being laid back. He was modest and less aggressive than his two assistants. He was firm and stable with no bit of discontent and appreciative of the help he received.

"They helped me," said Howell. "Vince wanted to have his own way, and he would shout and carry on. Tom never raised his voice, but he liked to have things his way, too. I'd have to referee some of that when their ideas clashed.

"One year the players were complaining that the practices were too long. I decided to cut them down. I called in the two of them and said, 'The players say you're working them too hard. I want you to give up a little time.' Vince said, 'Hell, I don't have enough time now.' And Tom said, 'Don't look at me. I'm not giving up anything if he isn't.' I'm not sure what we did, but we worked it out somehow.

"They were so opposite, it's almost funny. Lombardi seemed to know just about how far he could push a person. Tom didn't get mad the way Vince did. But he could get across with a look what Lombardi did with a roar."

There was little doubt that the Giants had one of the league's best coaching staffs. The players knew Landry and trusted him. However, when Lombardi arrived in 1956, he did so with some consternation. At Army, he was a proponent of the single wing, which featured a tailback to make it effective on a run-option play. There was no such formation in the NFL. Gifford was one of the first to get acquainted with Lombardi when he reported to training camp that year while he was still carrying his luggage.

"I saw Lombardi as I was walking into the dormitory," said Gifford. "He poked a finger at me, and his first words were, 'From now on you're my halfback.' I never played defense again. Lombardi believed in simplicity and total execution. Fancy things made him sick. But he always had a trick or two he could come up with.

"His first year with us he put in an option play with the quarterback sliding down the line of scrimmage. We had Charlie Conerly and Fred Benners, and between them they couldn't run a hundred yards in two minutes. Charlie would never call that play. Twice Vince sent me into the game with that play, and twice Charlie ignored him and called something else. Conerly was the only player that Vince never raised his voice to, not once.

"Really, we weren't quite sure what to make of him. He didn't look like a coach. He was coming in as a rookie as far as we were concerned. He gave us a lot of rah-rah and hand clapping, and we didn't take to that real well. The interesting thing is, Lombardi didn't let his ego get in the way of what he had to learn. He cut us some slack in doing it."

◆

By 1958 the Giants were a solid team that had won a championship just two years before. Their draft selections since returned dividends, and the trades they made were beneficial. In 1956 Sam Huff, Jim Katcavage, and Don Chandler became immediate starters as rookies. Getting Andy Robustelli from the Los Angeles Rams and Pat Summerall from the Chicago Cardinals completed the team's makeup. However, when the preseason games were unfolding, the Giants had lost five straight games after an opening game win. It certainly wasn't the right ingredient to intrude on the regular campaign. Ironically, the last two losses were inflicted by the Baltimore Colts.

The week before the regular season's opening game against the Cardinals in Chicago, Lombardi called for a team meeting at the Giants' home base, the Bear Mountain Inn. It wasn't met with any enthusiasm. The players were quite naturally expecting a tongue lashing for their poor play over the last five weeks. If anyone could vocalize the message with vigor, it was Lombardi.

"Everybody grumbled and cursed, but at 7:30 we showed up with our playbooks at our meeting room," said Jack Stroud, the team's star offensive guard. "One of the waitresses was standing there saying, 'The meeting is downstairs,' which was a rathskeller."

"Vince had a three-piece combo and kegs of beer. About 1:30 in the morning, he said, 'Okay, fellas, the party's over,' and everybody scrammed, filling as many of those gallon pasteboard containers to take them back to the dorm. Phil King grabbed a case of bottled beer, and when we got back, nobody had an opener. He smashed the bottle against the door jam and drank from the ragged edges. Only Phil could do that and not cut himself."

The Giants didn't exactly have a fortuitous schedule to embark on their championship quest, one they really wanted, after last season's disappointment. Their first three games were all on the road. The opener was in Chicago, of all places, because the Yankees were involved in still another World Series in their storied history, which the Giants would have loved to emulate. The Cardinals awaited them there, and before a slim crowd of 21,923, the Giants overcame the malaise they exhibited in dropping five straight exhibition games. Gifford assumed the leading role by scoring three touchdowns in a 37–7 rout. The 18 points he scored equaled the record by a Giants in a single game. The Giants had the game virtually won at halftime with a 27–7 advantage.

Gifford was the linchpin of the offense. If the Giants vowed to a man to make a championship run, they would need the offensive output represented by their versatile halfback. In the last three years, Gifford had led the Giants in total offensive yardage. Not many knew that he almost quit the team his rookie season of 1952 without even playing a game. He was packing his bags, ready to return to California, when Allie Sherman, an assistant coach, convinced him to stay. Gifford soon discovered that the Giants were an aging team that barely finished above .500 at 7–5. He had played more than anyone else, close to sixty minutes of football every game. Besides his offensive endeavors, he performed as a defensive back and even returned kickoffs. When the Giants floundered the following year with a 3–9 record, Gifford almost quit a second time.

"Pro football isn't what I thought it was going to be," he analyzed. "We can't beat anyone, and nobody's coming to the games. I'm getting killed, and I can make more than the eight thousand a year they're paying me. I didn't ever want to play this game again, and I seriously considered giving it all up."

Gifford felt the pain Kyle Rote was going through in rehabilitating his knee for two years. He had replaced him in the backfield because Rote had lost his speed. But Rote was a star quality player whom Wellington admired. In fact, he picked Rote ahead of Vic Janowicz, the Heisman Trophy–winning running back from Ohio State, in 1951. He was willing to wait on Rote for whatever it would take. The decision to move Rote to end saved his career, and Rote more than paid back the faith in him over the years he played.

Rote came to the Giants' doorstep by a stroke of the Maras' Irish luck. Just before the 1951 draft got under way, a local reporter trying to get a hint of who the Giants would pick asked Jack which player was sought above all the others.

"Kyle Rote of Southern Methodist," answered Jack.

"That's a ridiculous ambition," countered the journalist. "Rote is the number one player in the country, and he'll be long gone before your turn comes up."

"Who knows?" cheerfully responded Mara. "Maybe we'll get the bonus pick."

Mara was prophetic. Each team had a chance at the bonus pick by drawing a number out of a hat, in all probability Commissioner Bert Bell's chapeau.

"My brother Jack and I usually drew from the hat," explained Wellington. "But that year I said to him, 'Let's see if we can change our luck if Steve does the picking.' Owen pulled out the lucky ticket and the bonus pick that went along with it."

The Giants didn't have much luck their second week of the season in Philadelphia. They allowed the Eagles to upset them, 27–24, the first time they had beaten the Giants in six games. Gifford got the Giants' first touchdown, followed by Phil King's in the second quarter and Rote's diving end zone grab in the final one.

It was just that the Giants couldn't overcome the mastery of Eagle quarterback Norm Van Brocklin, who led the league in passing in 1950, 1952, and again in 1954. "The Dutchman," as he was called, completed sixteen of thirty-four passes for 238 yards and two touchdowns. He had Eagle fans screaming with a spectacular 91-yard touchdown pass to Tommy McDonald that gave Philadelphia a 17–10 second-quarter lead. Conerly matched Van Brocklin with two touchdown throws, but it wasn't enough, as Van Brocklin took the Eagles on a game-winning 66-yard drive in the closing minutes.

Against the Redskins, Conerly contributed with another two touchdown passes, which were the difference in the 21–14 victory. The winning toss was a dying duck, a ball that waffled in flight, but the thankful Giants were now 2–1 on a vital third-down play at the Washington 10-yard line. Conerly took the snap from center, faked a couple of handoffs, and ran to his left. Three Washington defenders chased him, and it didn't appear that Conerly could get any kind of a throw into the air. Miraculously, he did just before he hit the ground. The throw was intended for Gifford, but it floated over his head to Ken MacAfee.

The loss to the Cardinals was costly beyond the playing field itself. Gifford had been taken to St. Elizabeth Hospital at halftime with a severely injured knee, and the fear that accompanied it was that he could be sidelined as long as three weeks. He remained overnight, but the next morning, after the swelling had subsided, the prognosis was that there was minimal ligament damage. Gifford recalled a worse injury he incurred years earlier and was relieved that this latest one wasn't as damaging.

"In 1954, I hurt the same knee, although not in the same place, and I was out of action a couple of weeks," said Gifford.

"I didn't think this injury was as bad as that was. Anyway, I slept well, and aside from some soreness, the knee didn't feel that bad."

By the fifth week of the season, the Giants were at an early crossroads. They needed to assert themselves and win at least six of the next eight games to seriously contend for the Eastern banner. The game against the Pittsburgh Steelers was a pivotal one since the following week would be an encounter with the perennial powerhouse Browns in Cleveland. Their task against the Steelers was a dubious one. They would play their opponent in the rain and mud without Conerly, who had not missed a game since the 1956 season.

An alert defense went the extra yard in Conerly's absence. They created three fumbles, combined with an interception, holding the Steelers without a touchdown, the basis of a 17–6 required victory. Robustelli led a tenacious defense against Pittsburgh's Tom "The Bomb" Tracy, removing the ball from his clutches three times. Landry's unit also accounted for one of the two Giants touchdowns.

Acquiring Andy Robustelli from the Rams was one of the better trades in Giants history. He was a cerebral player from a school no one had ever heard of, Arnold College in upstate New York, one that didn't offer athletic scholarships. He was amazingly strong for a 220-pounder and had the knack to come up with the big play when one was needed. He was quick and agile enough to beat his bigger adversaries. Robustelli also brought a lot of passion to the game, and it was infectious to those around him. He carried that with him ever since he was raised in a poor immigrant family in Stamford, Connecticut.

"I was brought up in an integrated neighborhood," revealed Robustelli. "My father was a barber and my mother a dressmaker. We were very poor. I was born in a house where we were the only white family. There were four black families and us in this house.

"There were six kids in our family in a cold-water flat. All there was to do was play football, tackle in the street. We'd play football and baseball with a piece of rolled-up paper and put tape around it. I never got into trouble, but I was pretty close a few times.

"What saved me was the strong Italian family customs. Our parents were very strict, and we'd have to be in bed early, so there was only a certain amount of time you could get into trouble. We all lived around the church, which is probably what had the greatest influence on all us kids."

Robustelli had been a pro five years when the Giants traded for him in 1956. He was drafted by the Rams, and he admitted he never knew how the Rams learned about him. He was the only player ever drafted from Arnold. As a rookie in 1951, he replaced an injured Jack Zilly and started every game since.

"In '56, my wife was pregnant and almost due," remembered Robustelli. "It was summer, and I had to report. I called and asked if I could get about an extra five days to stay home. Sid Gillman was the coach, and he said no. He also said he'd fine me for every day I was late. Well, I told him I wasn't coming, and a few days later they traded me to the Giants for a number one pick."

That's when Wellington Mara got involved. He learned that the Rams had been soliciting offers for Robustelli. After he verified it with Los Angeles, he made a call to Robustelli.

"I've been talking to the Rams about you, and they're willing to trade you," remarked Wellington. "I know you are thirty years old, but do you think you could play two or three more years?"

"I'll try to play as long as I can, but I don't know how long that will be," answered Robustelli.

"If you tell me that you can play, or at least will try to play for that long, then I think I can make a trade for you," replied Wellington.

"Go ahead and make the deal," said Robustelli.

—

Facing the undefeated Browns in Cleveland was the season's biggest challenge. The Browns had already won all their games, and just about everyone had conceded them another Eastern title. The talk only invigorated the underdog New Yorkers, and before the day was over, the Giants would be back in contention. Conerly returned from his injury and provided the Giants with a clutch performance. He was everything a coach would expect, directing the offense with a minimum of flaws. He even used his imagination in bringing the Giants from behind at halftime to an inspiring 21–17 triumph by throwing three touchdown passes and removed the boos that hurt him in the opening home game at Yankee Stadium.

The largest crowd ever to see the Giants play, 78,404, witnessed the veteran Conerly's magic. He directed a 77-yard drive in a dozen plays, terminating it with a 15-yard touchdown pass to Alex Webster. With only 2:50 remaining to play, he again collaborated with the burly fullback on a game-clinching 10-yard touchdown, probably saving the season for the Giants. The defense supported Conerly magnificently. The Browns could only produce a paltry 27 yards in the second half, never crossing midfield, while Conerly was doing his number.

Conerly needed all the courage the human body could endure to keep playing at an advanced age. He was thirty-seven years old now and had the battle scars from his years of service with bad teams to remind him what it took to survive. He came to the Giants in 1948 as a single wing quarterback out of Mississippi. He started his rookie season, and after five years he was ready to quit football and return to a peaceful existence in Clarksdale, Mississippi. The Giants weren't very good under Conerly's watch, and he absorbed a physical beating far beyond the normal requisite.

But he was tough, was he ever. Marine tough. He served four years in combat on Guam, Iwo Jima, and Tarawa and had some close calls. With a weak offensive line and no noteworthy receiver, Conerly was at a distinct disadvantage and subjected to punishing tackles that caused him to leave the playing field aching after every game. He even played half of a season with a separated right shoulder, one of the most painful injuries anyone could absorb. That's how tough old Charlie was. After all he went through, Conerly hated to fail. But he had taken enough and wanted to retire. Only a persuasive Wellington Mara could get him to stay all these years by promising that he would give him a better offensive line and a receiver to go with it.

❧

The dramatic victory over the Browns electrified Giants fans. A record number of them, 71,163, showed up for the game at Yankee Stadium against Baltimore. The Colts, looking every bit like champion thoroughbreds, had won all six games they played. However, they would face the Giants without their star quarterback, Johnny Unitas, who was hospitalized with a collapsed lung. His loss created apprehension in a subdued Colts dressing room, and the Colts appeared a bit jittery when the Giants lined up on their first play from scrimmage.

The grizzled Conerly sensed it. He staggered the Colts with a daring play. He took center Ray Wietecha's snap, spun to his right, and tossed a lateral to Gifford, who flared wide and fired a 63-yard pass to end Bob Schnelker for a crowd-raising touchdown in setting the tone for what would result in a 24–21 win. Conerly and Rote then worked their magic. Rote informed him that he had set up Baltimore's defensive back Milt Davis for a fake. Rote ran straight at Davis, cut to the middle, then cut back again to the corner of the end zone. Conerly's pass was a trifle long, but the playmaking Rote left his feet and with a swanlike dive caught the ball and skidded on his head and shoulder and held on to the ball as he slid out of the end zone. The win lifted the Giants into a first-place tie with Cleveland.

Despite his age, which concerned many, Conerly was having a good season. He was making big plays, the type that could translate into a championship. And he took it all in stride without much emotion. He was a person of few words, often a "yup" or a "nope" characterizing his limited conversation. One could never tell if he had thrown a 50-yard touchdown pass or an interception. Yet he was a favorite of Gifford and Rote.

"Sometimes we'd go out, and Charlie wouldn't say anything for hours," revealed Rote. "But we knew he was having a good time because he didn't leave."

The following week the Giants suffered a damaging loss to the Steelers in Pittsburgh, 31–10, one that dropped them into second place. The defeat was as confounding as it was conclusive. The offense was nonexistent in producing only 191 yards. What created consternation was that the Giants jumped to a 10-0 lead, only to surrender 31 unanswered points. The bounce, the offensive zest, and the defensive drive that marked the wins over Cleveland and Baltimore were noticeably absent. The Giants had to go back to the drawing board.

❧

A cold first day of December kept the crowd away from Yankee Stadium. Only 35,438 showed up for the Eagles game, in which the Giants regained their winning edge, 24–10, to remain one game behind the Browns. The Giants led 17–10 at halftime and kept Philadelphia scoreless in the second half to secure the victory. It was the beginning of a December to remember. With Conerly sidelined, the Giants needed protection at quarterback. They moved swiftly and found little-known Jack Kemp of Occidental College in California and signed him to a contract. The future U.S. senator and vice presidential candidate never got to play, but he was a Giants nonetheless.

The final road game of the season took the Giants to Detroit. They would face an injury-depleted Lions team that was undermanned at several key positions. Yet they had to contain the passing and running of quarterback Tobin Rote and Detroit's speedy halfback, Gene Gedman. Before the game, Landry grabbed the arm of Jim Katcavage. "Don't forget," warned Landry. "You have to play wider than usual to guard against Rote and his rollout."

The safety the Giants recorded was a result of Landry's strategy. With the Lions on their 1-yard line, Katcavage was wide but knifed inside to spill Gedman for what turned out to be the difference in the score.

A bizarre ending provided the Giants with a 19–17 triumph. On fourth down and leading 17–12 and in possession on their own 44-yard line with 21 yards to go, even a poor punt would move the Lions out of danger. However, Detroit coach George Wilson ordered a fake punt. Yale Larry carried out the fake but barely got past the line of scrimmage. The Giants took advantage of the poor decision as Gifford scored the game-winning touchdown.

Still, the Lions had an opportunity to emerge victorious. Some eighty seconds before the end, Detroit had a field goal opportunity at the Giants 25-yard line. During a time-out, Robustelli and Svare discussed the best way to block Jim Martin's kick.

"I'll block the kick," announced Robustelli. "If you drive that guy inside, I can sneak through."

"Nothing doing," remarked Svare. "I'll block the kick. You'll have a better blocking angle than I will. You drive him inside."

"Okay," agreed Robustelli. "You block the kick."

Robustelli made his block, and Svare came crashing through with his arms upward. The ball struck him on the left wrist. The Giants escaped. A loss would have ended their season, falling behind two games with only one remaining.

❧

In a Hollywood backdrop, on a day actress Ingrid Bergman married Swedish movie producer Lars Schmidt in London, the Giants had a chance to play for the Eastern Division championship. With the Detroit win, they had remained one game behind Cleveland, and with a stroke of Mara luck, would face the Browns in Yankee Stadium. Snow was forecast and began falling a half hour before the kickoff. The chilling forecast kept some 10,000 fans away, which lowered the turnstile count to 63,192.

"Everyone is going to be stalled in this," observed Lombardi.

The Giants were well prepared for conditions like this and had victimized the Bears, which brought a championship on two occasions. However, this time the Giants had a major concern. Pat Summerall's injured right knee was bothering him in the pregame warm-ups. He practiced kicking field goals from various distances, and each kick brought a look of pain to his face. He honestly felt that he wouldn't be able to play.

"You better warm up," he told punter Don Chandler. "I don't think I'm going to be able to play."

It was the same familiar mission for the Giants defense, notably to contain Jim Brown, the NFL's premier runner. That primarily meant Huff shadowing his every move. Jack White had scouted the Browns the week before and didn't detect anything new in Brown's arsenal.

"There was nothing I could tell the coaches about the Browns and about Jimmy Brown that they did not already know," echoed White. "Jimmy is the greatest I have ever seen, and he certainly ranks among the greatest in professional football. He does so many things well."

The Giants and the Browns knew each other. In the nine times that Jim Lee Howell and Paul Brown had faced each other, the Cleveland mentor, regarded as the top strategist in the NFL, compiled a substantial 6–2–1 edge over the New Yorker. The last Giants win, 21–17, which occurred six weeks before, was still fresh in Brown's memory since nothing was more upsetting to him than losing at home before 80,000 fans, the largest venue in the league outside Los Angeles. He had that much pride and demonstrated as much when the Browns joined the NFL from the All America Football Conference. Ironically that season, the Browns defeated the Giants, 8–3, in a season-ending playoff game.

"We know we're faced with quite a test," said Brown. "They beat us at home, and they have the advantage of being on their home grounds. We know what we're faced with. For them to beat us twice is quite a chore. Well, you know, the Giants had a lot of breaks to get where they are. But you have to be lucky. Last year, you remember, luck was running with Detroit. This year it seems to be the Giants' turn."

Quarterback Milt Plum, in only his second year with the Browns, knew how much the game meant to Brown and was determined to atone for a poor performance in the loss to the Giants. For a youngster, he exuded confidence days before the crucial game.

"I believe we'll beat the Giants this time," announced Plum, which was quite an admission for someone who was reserved by nature. "I think our entire team believes we have the better club. I know I didn't have a good day when we lost to the Giants earlier this season. Some of the others told me that they had one of their worst days of the season, too."

The Giants didn't fare well in their opening possession. They began conservatively with three running plays that netted only a total of 4 yards. It was typical of their offensive strategy. Don Heinrich, instead of Charlie Conerly, would start the game and probe the Cleveland defense. It was frowned upon by Conerly, and he could never understand the thinking behind it.

"I never did know why they did that," remarked Conerly. "They would keep the ball on the ground. I didn't mind throwing it. They said Don would go in to see what the defense was doing, then come out and tell the coaches, and they'd change it up, and I'd go in. Didn't make much sense to me. You always see more when you're in there."

On Cleveland's very first play, Jim Brown made his imposing presence felt. Quarterback Milt Plum faked a pitchout to Lew Carpenter, which drew the Giants defense wide. He then gave the ball to Brown, who, with instant acceleration, got past the line of scrimmage when one of his tackles successfully sealed off Huff. When another Giants defender approached Brown, he accelerated again and sped into the secondary, past the defensive backs, and into daylight all the way into the end zone. The dynamic 65-yard journey stunned the Giants and their fans, 7–0.

New York's second possession produced some movement but nothing threatening. Heinrich did manage to reach the Cleveland 45 with a 15-yard third-down pass to Webster. However, when he needed to connect again on third down, he overthrew Gifford. Chandler sent a booming punt into the end zone, and Cleveland went on offense again from the 20-yard line.

Following a 2-yard gain, Plum quickly got the Browns moving with a 43-yard throw to Carpenter on the New York 35. The Giants needed a stop and responded by holding Brown to 5 yards on two runs. When Plum's pass to Ray Renfro failed,

Lou Groza attempted a 37-yard field goal that would give the Browns an early 10–0 lead. He stared at the goal posts after his kick sailed wide to the left.

Heinrich was finished after his two series, and the wily Conerly entered the game. Before the first quarter subsided, he had the Giants moving. It started with an 8-yard run by Webster from the Giants 15. Webster carried again, fumbled, but fortunately, Gifford recovered the ball on the 33. Conerly then connected with Schnelker for 11 yards and a first down on the 44.

Conerly came back to Schnelker when the second quarter began, which drew a pass interference penalty on Cleveland's 41-yard line. Two passes to Webster didn't work, and on a draw play Mel Triplett could only reach the 38. Howell sent in Summerall for a 46-yard field goal try. Summerall's leg wasn't strong enough, and his kick fell short.

With the snow falling steadily, the offense of both teams was affected. Neither came close to achieving a touchdown. The only attempts for points were by field goals. Summerall tried again and produced a 46-yarder that was the longest of his career. Groza matched him with one of 22 yards, which restored the Browns' 7-point lead, 10–3. He attempted one more in the closing seconds of the period and missed from 38 yards, which was very un-Groza-like. For an accomplished kicker who had earned the nickname "The Toe," he had missed two of the three field goals he tried.

The Giants escaped another threat when the second half began. The Browns took the kickoff, and Plum led them 54 yards to the New York 13. Groza was summoned for his fourth field goal attempt. Instead, he pulled a fake. Bobby Freeman, the holder, stood up and tried to pass. An alert Svare pinned him for a loss.

At halftime, Rote mentioned to Conerly that he detected something in the Browns secondary. "I noticed something," he said. "Maybe we can use it in the second half." Rote noticed that the secondary had overshifted to the right toward Gifford's run on the first-half pass. It wasn't until the final quarter that the Giants could exploit Rote's discovery. The opportunity arose after Robustelli recovered a Browns fumble on Cleveland's 35-yard line.

Conerly called the play that dispatched Gifford to the right, designating a run. As Rote had determined, the Browns secondary followed Gifford. Rote faked a block at the line of scrimmage and cut to the sideline. Gifford spotted him, stopped, and tossed a high, long pass diagonally across the field. Rote fiercely kept his eyes focused through the falling snow and came down with the ball on the Cleveland 6-yard line. It was a play of beauty, perfectly executed by the two cagey veterans.

Conerly didn't hesitate in calling for the tying touchdown. After a short run, he called for the same play, only this time Gifford delivered the ball to Del Shofner to deadlock the battle at 10–10. Cleveland needed only that outcome to clinch the division championship. They played it conservatively, taking time off the clock with their running game. The Giants played for the tie, too, clogging the line by setting up their linebackers close.

All the Giants needed was a field goal to force a playoff game the very next week. They were almost there, but Summerall was errant on a 38-yard try as the snow cascaded with intensity. As he trotted off the field, Huff remarked to the kicker, "We're going to give you another shot." Huff and the defense fulfilled their mission and stopped the Browns on three plays. They then succeeded in pressuring the punter, who shanked a punt around midfield.

Unfortunately, the Giants couldn't make a first down, although they almost made it on one play. Conerly heaved a perfect 50-yard pass to Webster in the end zone, and he dropped it.

There were just over two minutes left, and Howell had to make a vital decision: punt and hope that his defense would respond again, or attempt a field goal of some 50 yards in darkness and inclement weather with a sore-legged kicker. He ordered a field goal, and Summerall went out on the field again. Conerly was surprised.

"When we came onto the field, Conerly looked out of the huddle and snapped, 'What the hell are you guys doing here?'" disclosed Summerall. Conerly remained. He had to. As the holder, he had to clear out a spot to hold the ball for Summerall. A Cleveland time-out was signaled to add pressure to the Giants kicker.

"I didn't think about anything much when I went in," said Summerall. "I could have cried when I missed one just before, but all I thought about was that I would have to hit it good since it was a long kick. Then, when I was waiting for the snap, I kept reminding myself to lock my ankle. Sometimes I forget and let it waggle, but I remembered this time."

Conerly spotted the ball with the laces up, the way all kickers prefer. Summerall moved forward and made contact. The ball sliced like a golf ball as it took off, the trajectory to the right of the goal post. Then it curved and went accurately over the bar for the biggest field goal Summerall or the Giants had ever experienced. The kick was announced as 49 yards, but Summerall thought it went farther.

"No one knows how far it had to go," pointed out Summerall. "You couldn't see the yard markers. But it was more than 50 yards. I knew as soon as I kicked it that it was going to be far enough. I just couldn't believe Howell was asking me to do that. That was the longest kick I ever made."

In the Cleveland dressing room, Coach Brown, surrounded by reporters, was angry at a fourth-quarter call that went against him when the officials ruled that Gifford's dropped throw was an incomplete forward pass and not a fumble. He felt it cost him the game and the division championship.

"Look at them," he pointed in the direction of his weary players. "There isn't a man in this room who doesn't think that Frank Gifford fumbled that ball. I thought he made the catch, was hit, and fumbled it. Just as simple as that.

"The Giants thought he fumbled it. Did you see their defensive team? Some of them started out on the field thinking that Gifford had fumbled and the ball was ours. That was the big play. They wouldn't have won otherwise. They would never have scored, wouldn't have gotten close to kick that field goal."

Collecting himself, he also explained why he ordered a fake field goal in the third quarter from the Giants 12-yard line with the Browns ahead 10–3.

"We wanted the touchdown," he emphasized. "It would have made it that much harder for them to win. The big seven would have broken the game open. If we had scored the touchdown, they would have to score two touchdowns to tie. We were willing to settle for a tie. That would have given us the title. They had to win to stay alive, and two touchdowns at that point was a large order.

"The guy who threw our runner for the loss was decoying one of our blockers out of the play, so no other lineman could get in to try to block the kick."

Since their upset loss to the Steelers in November, the Giants had burdened themselves by having to win each Sunday to remain only a game behind Cleveland. Howell appeared calm at what he had just experienced.

"How can a guy get excited the way we've been playing 'em the last few weeks?" he asked. "Next week? I don't know. This is a great team emotionally. But how many times emotionally can you do this?"

Howell would find out. The Giants would play another game.

Quarterback Johnny Unitas of the Baltimore Colts drops back to pass during the NFL Championship Game on December 28, 1958, against the New York Giants at Yankee Stadium in New York. It was the first overtime game in NFL history, and the first game to be nationally televised.

Kidwiler Collection/Diamond Images/Getty Images

Giants Key Players *(left to right from top)*: Sam Huff; Andy Robustelli; Charlie Conerly; Alex Webster; Emlen Tunnell.

Photos courtesy of Giants organization

Colts Key Players *(left to right from top)*: Alan Ameche; Raymond Berry; Art Donovan; Gino Marchetti; Lenny Moore; Jim Mutscheller; Johnny Unitas; Steve Myhra (left) and Jim Parker.

Photos courtesy of Colts organization

Receiver Raymond Berry of the Baltimore Colts locks in on a pass from Unitas in the championship game. Unitas passed for 349 yards, and Berry had 12 receptions for 178 yards.

Baltimore Colts defensive end Gino Marchetti watches the game from the sideline with a broken leg suffered on his game-saving tackle of Frank Gifford late in the fourth quarter.

Pro Football Hall of Fame/Getty Images

Running back Alan Ameche of the Baltimore Colts tries to break through the New York Giants defenders Dick Modzelewski (77), Emlen Tunnell (45), and Sam Huff (70) en route to the Colts overtime victory.

Kidwiler Collection/Diamond Images/Getty Images

Alan Ameche lowers his shoulder and charges over the goal line to score the game-winning touchdown. Colts 23, Giants 17.

Pro Football Hall of Fame/Getty Images

Top, left to right: Raymond Berry, Johnny Unitas, and Lenny Moore of the Baltimore Colts. *Bottom, left to right:* Frank Gifford, Charlie Conerly, and Kyle Rote of the New York Giants.

Pro Football Hall of Fame/Getty Images

COLTS 1958 SEASON

Fulfillment

The dawn of the 1958 season generated a euphoric transformation never before experienced in the sardonic nine interrupted years that professional football was played in Baltimore. The reason? Johnny Unitas. In 1957, only his second year as a pro, Unitas provided hope for the locals when he led the Colts to a 7–5 record, their first winning season in the team's history. He arrived in Baltimore in 1956 off the Pittsburgh sandlots, hardly a ringing endorsement, especially for one who was literally a nobody. It was a persona he carried with him ever since his high school days at St. Justin's High School, a ½-mile walk from his home. Nobody wanted a skinny, slightly bowlegged kid, and in all those frustrating years, Unitas quietly harbored his feelings without so much as a whimper.

As a courtesy to all the high school kids who played in Pittsburgh and its environs, which was a hotbed of football, his hometown Steelers drafted him on the ninth round of the 1954 draft, which, for a quarterback prospect, was practically an obituary. In the six exhibition games that year, Unitas humbly stood on the sidelines in each one of them, never once getting the chance to take a single snap from center to show that he was indeed a member of the team and could throw an efficient forward pass. He knew it would never happen when Ted Marchibroda joined the Steelers the last week of training camp following his Army discharge, which gave the Steelers four quarterbacks, one too many. Unitas was unceremoniously released and generously given $10 bus fare home from Olean, New York, but not before he had something to say to the Steelers head coach.

"I don't mind if you gave me the opportunity to play and I screwed up, but you never gave me the opportunity," Unitas tersely pointed out to Walt Kiesling.

If he didn't get a contract, he at least took the money. He stuffed the $10 in his pocket and hitchhiked home. Unitas had a parting shot about his summer of discontent once he got back to Pittsburgh.

"I'm sure he didn't realize I was in camp until the Associated Press ran a picture of me showing a Chinese nun how to throw a football," remarked the now unemployed Unitas.

Unitas may not have heard of Diogenes or anyone else in Greek mythology, but he certainly could relate. When Diogenes was discovered begging money from a statue, he explained that he was "practicing disappointment." That may well have been Unitas, who knew the meaning of the word *disappointment* at every level, from high school to reaching the pros. All he wanted was a chance.

⬢

Baltimore coach Weeb Ewbank could easily empathize with Unitas. Ewbank was beginning his final season with the Colts with an ominous cloud over his head. In four years under his stewardship, Ewbank had produced a vanilla 20–27–1 record. Owner Carroll Rosenbloom had a penchant for gambling, and in his eyes Ewbank clearly wasn't winning enough.

Unitas and Ewank had a special bond ever since that April day in 1956 when the veteran coach observed the inexperienced youngster throw in a tryout at a Baltimore park. It was Ewbank's recommendation to the team's general manager, Don Kellett, that got Unitas a $7,000 contract to play for the Colts and for the first time in his football life, Unitas felt wanted.

Several months later Ewbank saw Unitas again in training camp, and within a week knew he had someone special. He admired Unitas's arm strength and touch, but he also detected something peculiar with Unitas's delivery. He didn't say anything, but when he viewed film the next day, he was amazed and at the same time surprised no one had ever made mention of it.

"When he followed through, his fingers turned over, and you could see the back of his hand," exclaimed Ewbank. "I wondered how he kept from injuring his arm because it was like throwing a screwball, and all those guys would end up with a crooked arm.

"With his tremendous follow-through, he would often snag his fingernails on the back of a guy's shirt and jam his fingers like on one of his own linemen. I worried that he might get what they call a tennis elbow, but, boy, I saw the way he could throw, and I never worried about it. You knew right away. He was in camp in no time at all, and we all knew that as soon as he learned the offense, he would be our quarterback."

Now, more than ever, Ewbank needed Unitas. The final two weeks of the 1957 season were especially nettlesome to Ewbank. The Colts rode west carrying a 7–3 record and primed to win the Western Division championship in Unitas's first full season as quarterback. They were cogent with a four-game winning streak in which they averaged 27 points a game. In the last two games, they defeated San Francisco, 27–21, and Los Angeles, 31–14, in closing their regular season schedule in Baltimore.

They arrived in San Francisco with a one-game lead over the 49ers, needing a victory to clinch at least a share of the title. However, they lost a tough 17–13 struggle against the Niners, then fell completely apart the following week against the Rams in Los Angeles, 37–21. It rankled a seething Rosenbloom, who was there in person for what he anticipated would be a celebratory trip.

On their return flight to Baltimore, the players suspected that Ewbank wouldn't be their coach in 1958. A week later, Ewbank's fears were realized in a private meeting with Rosenbloom that didn't last long. Rosenbloom didn't mince words in declaring to Ewbank that 1958 would be his final year unless he won a championship. And he gave the beleaguered coach an edict: Be tougher on the players.

⬤

During the off-season, Unitas didn't dwell on what could have been. He never looked back. The first thing he did was to work as a salesman for a paint company in Baltimore at $200 a week to support his wife and two kids. All he knew at the time was that the strong yet disappointing 1957 season saved Ewbank's job.

When Unitas reported to camp, Ewbank pulled him aside.

"John, I can't tell you how important this season is for me," confided Ewbank. "I'm going to count on you more than ever. That's all I can say for now."

The stoic Unitas was the substance, not the hype. Despite appearing in only twenty games, he was looked upon as the deliverer. In his first year he was the NFL's rookie of the year and in 1957 the league's player of the year. Ewbank had to feed off his quarterback if he wanted to succeed and keep his job. Unitas knew the gravity of the situation between Rosenbloom and Ewbank. He harbored support for his coach.

"I liked Weeb and always got along with him," disclosed Unitas. "I truly enjoyed playing for him because he left me alone to call my own plays. That is, except the first three plays of every game. Weeb always gave me the first three plays like clockwork every Saturday night. There were times when I had to check off during a game because I knew a run up the middle would never work, and I'd switch to a pass play. When it worked for a touchdown, Weeb would holler to us coming off the field, 'See? I told you it would work.' I just shook my head and smiled."

Despite his short, squatty appearance that gave him the look of a leprechaun with a crew cut, he was a better coach than most people gave him credit. Weeb's strength was in his organization, no doubt a trait he inherited when he worked for Paul Brown in Cleveland for five years. He also knew that the strength of any team was its veteran players, and he wisely took care of them and practically left them on their own, offering a word of encouragement almost every day. If he wanted to exert his authority and illustrate a point, he would always pick on a rookie. That was his way.

"I was thinking one night, and as I did, I began chuckling to myself," recalled Unitas. "We were a team nobody wanted. I was a quarterback no other team wanted, we had a coach that the owner really didn't want, and I'm thinking we can win a championship. We were truly a team of football orphans that found a home together."

When the Colts reported to training camp that summer at Western Maryland College in Westminster, a pastoral hamlet 30 miles from Baltimore, they immediately detected a change in Ewbank's persona the very first day. Ewbank assembled his players and demanded more discipline from the year before, and he especially exhorted his veteran players. He announced that he would impose a $100 fine that went with a dressing down for anyone reporting late on the field or at team meetings.

He had the perfect foil in Alan Ameche. In previous years, if Ameche or Gino Marchetti or even the team's clown, Art Donovan, walked in late for a meeting, Ewbank wouldn't say a word. However, if a rookie did it, the stubby Ewbank would jump a foot off the ground and fine the frightened player a hundred bucks.

Ameche loved to play cards. He would sit in his dormitory room day after day and play every last hand he could before rushing off to practice. Often, dealing one more hand caused him to be late for practice. Nothing severe, perhaps five minutes or so. The times that he was late were borderline. He just liked to play games with Weeb and wasn't concerned that Coach would change his easygoing manner and turn into a tyrant.

This year was different, and Rosenbloom's constant appearances at practice served as a reminder to Ewbank, only to be deferred by Ameche. The big fullback maintained his habits, only this time Ewbank began to yell at him in front of the other players and slap him with a $100 fine. It never bothered Ameche, who continued his card playing and regularly increased the players' fine pool, which meant there'd be a bigger party at the end of the season.

Weeb's first visible discipline of a veteran player like Ameche was his way of impressing Rosenbloom and the entire team that he expected nothing short of a championship. He had to demonstrate to the owner that the atmosphere in training camp had dramatically changed from past years. Down deep, Ewbank knew he had a team that could win a championship. They came close last season. Yet he wasn't comfortable changing his personality. He never explained his actions to Ameche, but he did so to Unitas to clear the air.

"John, I have to do that to Ameche," he confessed. "I've got to make him realize where it's at so he can play all out."

"You don't have to do that," Unitas assured him. "Ameche is a player. He's always there when the whistle blows."

Ewbank loved Ameche like a son, even though he made him his whipping boy that summer. Because of Ameche's personality, he knew he could get away with doing so. Below his rugged appearance he was a soft-hearted person. But on a football field, he was a fierce competitor who could inflict a hurt on a defensive player.

"Once during a game last year, Ewbank got on Ameche's butt, imploring him to run harder," recalled Unitas. "The next time Ameche got the ball, he broke loose down the sidelines. He got bumped out of bounds, and to cushion his fall, he came down with his fist on a table and broke it in half. Weeb came running over all excited and yelled to everyone around, 'See what I made him do!'

"Ameche was like a bull with a flower in his mouth. I went over to his house one night and heard opera music blaring over the stereo.

"'I didn't know you were an opera lover,' I remarked.

"'I love the stuff,' said Ameche, 'but nobody knows about it.'

"Driving home that night I wondered if Ameche would ever play his opera music in the dressing room for all the players to hear. Donovan would have a ball with it."

Training camp was tougher than ever before under Weeb. Not only did he have the players working twice a day, but he kept them occupied with meetings, keeping them focused on what their mission was in limiting their free time. Nowhere was Ewbank's organizational ability more evident than through the playbook. He would stand in front of a blackboard and read everything to the players, word by word, like a minister with a Bible.

"It seemed like we were back in school," said Unitas. "He made us take notes, too. We had to sit for hours at a time and write such coaching fundamentals for a crackback block, shoulder block, and even a downfield block. I couldn't believe what was going on. All I wanted to know was the pass routes of my receivers and the hole my running backs had to go through.

I had to know all the responsibilities of everyone else on the team.

"Weeb was serious alright. Yet, at the same time, he was making all of us better players. He felt strongly about the fact that you learned from reading, writing, and studying. And damned if he didn't grade us from time to time! He actually gave us examinations. We were back in school alright."

—

None of this bothered Art Donovan, the team's mammoth defensive tackle, who found a way to make it to the Silver Run Inn in Silver Run, Maryland, some nights. He was the resident comic who took delight in any prank anyone would eschew. Most of the time he would create them. He was a street-smart guy from the Bronx who fought with the Marines in the Pacific and had been all-everything in high school football, specifically All-Metropolitan and All-City Catholic. However, he was far from a model Catholic student, being as mischievous as a kid could be without getting into any serious trouble. He began with the Colts in 1950, and he was so big they weighed him on a grain scale, 6 feet, 2 inches, 300-plus pounds. He called himself a light eater.

"When it got light, I started eating," mused Donovan.

He always had a clause in his contract that dictated he must be in shape to play at 270 pounds. That, too, never bothered him, and he was as happy-go-lucky as they came.

"I never watched my weight. I always knew where it was," said Donovan, laughing. "One spring I gave up beer and baloney for Lent and just made the 270-pound limit."

It wasn't only that Donovan had a voracious appetite, like four double cheeseburgers as a snack, but he also never met a Schlitz he wouldn't drink. It all had to do with his Irish family background, where beer was the preferred beverage for both his grandfather and father, who were professional boxers, and a couple of uncles who were inspectors in the New York Police Department. It was a close-knit Irish brood that would always gather at the grandmother's apartment every Sunday, and Donovan was so good at football that he received a scholarship from Notre Dame, which was every Irish kid's dream but Donovan's.

"I didn't really want to go, but my mother made me," lamented Donovan. "My first and only football love was the Fordham Rams."

Donovan didn't exactly get along with Notre Dame coach Frank Leahy and lasted only a semester at South Bend. Leahy told Donovan that he wasn't his type, whatever that meant. Donovan never did figure it out. It didn't matter much anyway because Donovan ended up enlisting in the Marines, which didn't go over too well with his father. He remembered his dad yelling at his mother, "Kiss him goodbye, Mary, he's going to get killed. He's going to get his fat ass shot right out from under him." After two years in the Pacific, Donovan came back unharmed and enrolled at Boston College.

Gino Marchetti, who lined up next to Donovan, was also a war veteran. More than that, he was a hero who took part in the Battle of the Bulge that turned the tide of the war for the Allies. The war was personal for Gino. His family had emigrated from Italy to West Virginia and ultimately settled in Antioch, California. When the war broke out, the government ordered his mother to relocate, restricting her movements because she was lacking citizenship papers. Italians who had not completed the naturalization process were considered enemy aliens. When he got out of high school at eighteen, Marchetti enlisted in the Army, and his heroic exploits earned him medals and a reprieve for his mother.

"You have no idea how much those immigrants worshipped the USA and the chance to be in this country," recalled Marchetti. "We tried to boost my mom's spirits all the time, but for six months she must have cried every day. My family loved America, and my older brother and I were ready to die in the war. We accepted what happened because we believed in obeying orders. If we were told to do something like that, my father said there must be a good reason. So we did it without a word of complaint.

"As the war wound down in Europe, we must have been taking 5,000 prisoners a week. The Germans were down to rock bottom, kind of like that Dallas Texans team I played on in 1952 before coming to Baltimore."

Along with Donovan, he was there from the beginning and at 6 feet, 4 inches, 244 pounds became a force. He was adept at stopping the run along with being a vicious pass rusher. Marchetti, in fact, introduced the concept of an end pressuring the quarterback, which he did with demonic fervor. With a high threshold for pain, he once played half a game with a separated shoulder and another two weeks after an appendectomy.

"He's the greatest player in football," praised Rams head coach Sid Gillman. "It's a waste of time to run around this guy's end. It's a lost play."

—◦—

There was something about the atmosphere at training camp that was definitely different from past years. Despite Ewbank's mandate, the players appeared loose and confident and at the same time in a playful mood. The 1957 season did that. Every player on the team felt they could win now after coming the closest they ever did in the final two weeks of the season. The Colts had demonstrated balance with a productive offense that averaged 25.3 points a game and a rigid defense that allowed 19.7 points in finishing their year's work at 7–5. They were anxious to report to training camp for the 1958 campaign.

"I couldn't wait to get here," confessed Marchetti. "It means getting together with all the guys."

The Colts were a tightly knit bunch. Their fans looked upon them with the same fervor that the nation's teens were screaming over Elvis Presley. Being beloved underdogs created the bonding among the players. The camaraderie seemed even more abundant this year. They had a caring owner in Carroll Rosenbloom, who took a sincere effort in his players' welfare off the field. But Weeb Ewbank, whom the owner once described as "my crew cut IBM machine," was in trouble, and the players surmised as much. Ewbank was now one of them. It even reached a point where Don Kellett asked some of the players if Ewbank should be fired.

"You're asking me, a player, if a coach should be fired?" responded Art Donovan. "What, are you crazy?"

The grizzled Donovan was the most unmistakable character in the locker room, as well as being one of the most respected. With an insatiable appetite, he did all he could to maintain the 270-pound demand Ewbank inflicted on him. He decided the best way was to cut down on the cold cuts—at least until the baloney appeared. Donovan was a favorite among his teammates and a natural target for the mischievous pranks that prevail at training camp. He had a fear of furry animals, which made him an easy victim for the capriciousness of others.

There was a night the unsuspecting Donovan was notably victimized. He pulled down the covers of his dormitory bed and screamed aloud at a dead groundhog. He went out yelling every expletive he knew while looking for another place to sleep. The next day, when Donovan reported for practice, he erupted again. He opened his locker and discovered that the same groundhog that was lying in his bed was hanging from a rope. He turned and ran out of the room, knocking over an attendant on the way out.

Jim Parker was also a frequent victim. He always cautiously looked into his locker after practice, afraid of what he might find. Objects like snakes, small animals, even chicken feet, were common discoveries. "He'd go through his clothes and find something moving, and he'd jump all over the place," exclaimed Lenny Lyles, the Colts' number one draft pick that year.

Even Marchetti, a serious, no-nonsense individual, would occasionally get in on the fun.

"One day after practice we were fooling around," began Marchetti. "Taseff wanted to get Ameche. So he filled a bucket of water and waited around the corner of the building until I signaled him that Ameche was coming. I saw Weeb Ewbank all dressed up, and just as he walked through the door, I gave Carl the signal. The funniest part was watching how Carl tried to chase after the water and catch it in the bucket before it hit Weeb."

The carefree antics were a welcomed diversion from the dull existence that infected the players at camp. There wasn't any entertainment they could fall back on and why, indeed, they provided it with self-induced horseplay. Johnny Sample, a rookie defensive back from Maryland State, found out as much his first week.

"There wasn't much to do around here," admitted Sample. "After dinner Gene Lipscomb and I usually went to shoot a little pool. The guy let us shoot free until we had to get back to the dorm. There just wasn't anything else to do."

The Colts unleashed their pent-up frustrations in their first preseason game against the Philadelphia Eagles in Hershey, Pennsylvania. A heated dispute took place followed by fisticuffs, which never occurs in such meaningless games. Eagle quarterback Norm Van Brocklin stood next to Don Joyce, the Colts rugged defensive end, and remarked, "Listen, champ, if a fight starts, I'm on your side."

Two weeks later, against Washington in Baltimore, Buzz Nutter was having a difficult time containing Redskins guard Jim Ricca. During a time-out, he discussed the situation with Ewbank. "What can we do with this Ricca?" asked Ewbank. "Hell, Weeb, I think you ought to trade for him," suggested Nutter.

When the preseason ended, the Colts had played six games and finished 2–3–1, hardly a portend of what was to come. If there were an omen, it was that they played the Giants in the last two games and won them both. Baltimore was a hungry team brimming with big anticipation of the approaching season. So were their frantic fans. For the third successive year, the Colts established a new season ticket sale that had reached 30,179. The painful three last-minute defeats to Detroit, San Francisco, and Los Angeles still weighed on the players' minds. They were three games they should have won but let them slip away, and no one was more anxious for the 1958 season to begin than Unitas.

"As we approached the regular season, I felt confident that we could win a title," confided Unitas. "The players felt the same way. It was up to me to lead them, a team that was good enough to win a championship. I was getting itchy knowing that we could win it all. I couldn't wait for the season to start."

His reliable tight end, Jim Mutscheller, felt the same way. He was almost overlooked in the Colts' high-octane attack, but he was one of Unitas's favorite receivers, whom he often looked to in clutch third-down throws.

"I could see more things falling in place each season," pointed out Mutscheller. "We had a good draft in 1955, and then we picked up Unitas and Lenny Moore. By 1958 it just seemed that it was our time."

Berry was every bit as confident. He looked back at the 1957 season that ended so frustratingly.

"We had a good team, but we just didn't have the knowledge that we could win," said Ray Berry. "It hadn't dawned on us how good we really were. We went to California needing to win, and we lost because we didn't think of ourselves as being champions. It happens to young teams very often. They need a year of learning they can win before they do win."

Berry's words were prophetic. It appeared that the Colts had indeed learned, galloping for six straight wins, the longest in club history. It was the platinum combination of Unitas and Berry that got them started in the very first game against the Lions at home. Baltimore had to rally after falling behind, entering the fourth quarter to salvage a 28–15 victory. Unitas and Berry rhapsodized for ten completions that generated 149 yards and two touchdowns. Unitas finished with twenty-three of forty-three for 250 yards. He was also the center of a key defensive play. Detroit defensive end Bob Long intercepted him on the 33-yard line and started for the end zone. Unitas, ever the competitor, brought down Long on the 10-yard line to save a touchdown. The defense, inspired by Unitas's effort, stuffed the Lions and kept them off the scoreboard. Unitas then quickly took the Colts for the first of two game-winning touchdowns.

Berry was the epitome of a perfectionist. There wasn't anybody in the league like him, except Unitas. It was Berry who encouraged Unitas to stay those long hours after practice and work on timing and routes like two ballet dancers. They had worked like this for two years in perfecting their art and were now well tuned to contribute to a championship. Each had earned the respect of their teammates, maybe not the first time they were scrutinized as rookies in 1956, but ever since.

"Everybody wondered what the hell Berry was doing here," said Ameche. "He had one leg shorter than the other, wore contact lenses, was barely 185 pounds, didn't have speed, and wasn't particularly strong. But just from hard work he made it.

"He'd drive John crazy keeping him out after practice. John would call a masterful game, but it was really the perfection of Raymond as a player that made it work. The amazing thing about Raymond is that these were not lucky things. He worked on these. He not only accented the things he could do well and tried to improve on them, but he'd think of the exceptions, like the ball that's thrown behind you and the one that's down on the ground or thrown too high. The thing I always admired about Raymond was that he never thought anything was impossible."

Berry actually looked out of place in the locker room. He never was gifted with prolike athleticism and had a shy look about him. He needed a corset for a bad back, was nearsighted, and possessed only average speed. He designed his own shoes to compensate for his shorter leg. But he had determination and creativity that amazed everyone with his attention to detail and confounded offensive backs with his precision moves. He studied films at home and caught passes from his wife in the backyard, which all added to the Berry mystique.

"When I saw a movie about Elroy "Crazylegs" Hirsch, I thought, I sure wish I could catch passes like that guy," revealed Berry. "Then, when I got to Baltimore, I was just trying to stay around one year. I never would have made it if it wasn't for Ewbank. He saw something in me, and Unitas, too, when neither of us had any reputation or track record.

"What I had to do was learn moves and finesse techniques to get open. I learned my moves from watching other receivers. I studied every film I could get. You got to be able to get open and catch the ball. I had good hands and could catch the ball, and I had a great quarterback throwing to me. Unitas was such a tremendous passer, so accurate with a good release. If there was just a little crack, he'd get the ball in."

Berry was every inch the perfectionist. During a game in 1957, Ewbank wanted to capitalize on a weakness he spotted in the opposition's secondary. During a time-out, he explained a play to both Unitas and Berry.

"This should give us a touchdown," enthused Ewbank in explaining the play.

"I'm sorry, but I can't do it," remarked Berry.

"Why not?" asked Ewbank.

"Because I haven't practiced it," countered Berry.

Unitas just shook his head. He had the ultimate respect for Berry, and no two players were closer.

"After throwing to him those first two years, I knew he'd be a great one," observed Unitas. "I never saw an athlete so dedicated. He was a self-made star. He had no speed, ran the 40 in 4.8 or 4.9. But he had uncanny moves and worked on them all the time. Everything had to be precise. He would come in on a Monday morning after a Sunday game and look at film of the team we were playing next. Then on Tuesday, when we reported back for practice, he'd have a yellow pad with a list to show me.

"'John, these are the things I can do against this guy we're playing Sunday,' Berry would point out. 'I can give him the inside move or to the outside like this. I'll let you know when I can do it.'

"Often during a game he'd come back into the huddle, and he'd say something to me like, 'I've got a five-step inside move on the 20.' I would then set the offense to occupy different people to make sure he ended up in single coverage. If the defense changed coverages on me, then I'd just go somewhere else with the ball.

"Berry never stopped working to improve. I'd throw extra to him after practice, anywhere from forty-five minutes to an hour every day. He was so dependable I'd never have to worry about throwing to him in a game. He used to beat everybody. During a preseason game in Miami, we knocked the hell out of Pittsburgh. Later at the airport, we were all there, the Colts and the Steeler players, and I was talking to Bobby Layne. Berry came walking through the concourse, and Layne spotted him.

"God damn, no wonder he can get open," exclaimed Layne. "He's got moves when he walks."

"I never saw a more easygoing guy. Nothing ever fazed him. When he'd go to sleep at night or take a nap, he'd shut out everything by putting those black blinders over his eyes. Berry was also very religious, and we all respected him for that. One time in Detroit we were all sitting on a bus that would take us to the stadium. Raymond was the last one out of the hotel. As he came toward the bus, a panhandler approached him and asked him for some money.

"Raymond reached into his pocket, took out three one-dollar bills, and gave them to the guy. He looked at Raymond like he was goofy. As he started to walk away, Berry grabbed his arm and pulled the startled guy back toward him. Raymond then took out his Bible and read a verse from it. What a scene. The guy just stood there and listened, probably hoping Berry wouldn't take the three dollars back. When he had finished, Raymond stuck the Bible back into his pocket and walked on the bus. Nobody said a word."

Unitas once more proved the difference the following week on a 51–38 caging of the Bears before 52,622 happy fans in Memorial Stadium. Instead of Berry, Lenny Moore shared the spotlight with the quarterback as the Colts stampeded to a 27–3 first-quarter lead. When the game ended, Moore had scored four touchdowns on runs of 28 and 9 yards and two others on passes of 77 and 33 from Unitas. Leonard Lyles, from Unitas's alma mater, Louisville, showed his speed in returning a kickoff 103 yards for a touchdown. An amazing quirk was that, although the Bears were intercepted five times, they did manage to score 38 points.

Moore was performing with all the pent-up fury from his childhood. He was one of a poor black family of eleven in Reading, Pennsylvania, where his father worked in the steel mill and his mother as a domestic. He was recruited by Rip Engle at Penn State, where he ran with speed that got him $10,000 as the Colts' first-round pick in 1957. His family was supportive of Moore in college, and he never forgot receiving $2 in the mail every week from his mother and clothes on occasion from his brothers.

Two dollars was big money for Moore. "I knew my mom couldn't afford it," Moore recalled. "It was floor-scrubbing money. Where else would she get it? It's something I'll never forget."

When Moore arrived in Baltimore his rookie season, he discovered that he couldn't go to any of the movies downtown because he was black. It was the same at restaurants, and it rankled him. He was forced to live in a black area in northwest Baltimore. Moore thought that once he got to Baltimore, it would be different than it was at Westminster. There were two movies in town at the training camp, and he couldn't go to either one. Take-out food was all he could get from a restaurant. He couldn't even go for a beer with the white players. The football field was where he released his anger.

❧

The Colts displayed remarkable resiliency by staking the Packers to a 17–0 advantage in Milwaukee in their first road game of the young season. Unitas managed to lead them back in the second half with a 54-yard touchdown strike to Mutscheller.

With less than five minutes remaining and behind 17–14, Unitas was carrying the Colts toward a go-ahead touchdown when he fumbled on the Packers 8-yard line. Linebacker Ray Nitschke recovered for Green Bay, or so he thought. Referee Bob Austin ruled he had blown his whistle before Unitas lost the ball.

On fourth down, Myhra came through with a 14-yard field goal to give the Colts a 17–17 tie. It allowed an alert Baltimore secondary to capitalize on quarterback Bart Starr's mistake. Starr, who was having a huge game, completing twenty-six of forty-six passes for 320 yards, was errant on a critical throw. Defensive back Andy Nelson picked him off and ran 52 yards for the winning touchdown, 24–14, with only 1:12 left on the clock. After the game, there was a noticeable sigh of relief in the Colts dressing room.

"We stuck our hands right in the blaze, right in the red hot coals, and pulled it out," exclaimed Don Joyce as he was removing the tape from his ankles. "That's just what we did."

Three straight wins created a buzz around Baltimore. Yet it was tempered somewhat by the realization that the Colts never played well in Detroit, especially with fourth-quarter collapses. Blowing a 27–3 fourth-quarter lead to the Lions last year was a painful memory that the Colts carried into this year's game. They erased it. The Colts broke open a close game with 20 last-quarter points for a 40–14 whipping.

The triumph not only kept the Colts on top of the Western Division, but it equaled the longest wining streak they ever had. It was a concerted team effort. Moore delivered 136 yards in twelve carries as Baltimore accumulated a total of 535. The defense made its presence felt, too, by holding the Lions to only 79 yards on the ground.

The season's largest crowd, 54,403, poured through the turnstiles at Memorial Stadium for the contest against the hated Redskins. A 7–0 Washington lead was quickly eradicated by Lyles. This time he returned a kickoff 101 yards for the tying touchdown and with it entered the NFL record books. He was the first to produce touchdown runs of more than 100 yards twice in a single season. It sparked the Colts to a 35–17 romp.

Unitas, with touchdown passes of 17 and 48 to Berry, passed Sid Luckman and joined Lyles in the record books by throwing a touchdown pass in twenty consecutive games; he only threw fifteen passes the entire game. The players awarded the game ball to Nutter, who played against doctors' orders with three cracked ribs. "We couldn't match the Colts bench, and when you can't do that, you're in trouble," moaned Washington owner George Preston Marshall, who had offended the players with some testy remarks at a luncheon earlier in the week. "We got the hell beat out of us."

By now Colts fans were raising hell over a 5–0 Colts performance. A driving rainstorm couldn't keep 51,333 away from the Green Bay game. The Packers wished they had stayed away after absorbing a 56–0 bludgeoning. It was the first ever shutout by a Baltimore team.

It was a costly win, however. The Colts were ahead 20–0 in the closing minutes of the first half when Unitas broke loose on a 14-yard run to the Packers 6-yard line. Defensive back John Symank speared Unitas and left him in pain, holding his ribs. Unitas had to be helped off the field and was taken directly to the locker room. George Shaw took over and completed 10 of 13 passes to ensure the victory. Once again the secondary registered five interceptions as seven different Colts scored touchdowns.

Unitas's injury was serious, much more than anyone anticipated. He was transported to Union Memorial Hospital the morning after the game. The fractured ribs had punctured a hole in Unitas's lung, which required emergency surgery. There were even rumors that he received last rites of the Catholic

Church. Unitas was dismayed about his future, a broken quarterback with a punctured lung. Would he be able to ever play again?

Two days later the operation equipment man, Dick Spassoff, and trainer Eddie Block visited Unitas, carrying a football in their hands, which left a puzzled look on Unitas's face. Their intentions were noble. They wanted to allay Unitas's worst fear that he couldn't throw a football anymore. Heavily bandaged, Unitas sat up in bed and took the ball in his hands. He gripped it softly and brought a smile to everyone's face, including his own, with a well-thrown pass.

The unbeaten Colts were 6–0, but could they win without Unitas? There were reports that he would be sidelined as long as six weeks. A worried braintrust, Rosenbloom, Kellett, and Ewbank, decided to reach out to Gary Kerkorian again. This time he wasn't in Washington but 3,000 miles way in California. Kerkorian was now a practicing attorney in Inglewood and after conferring with the Colts management presented them with a favorable case. He would make himself available for Sunday games but would only practice on Thursday and Friday before returning to the West Coast on Sunday night.

It was up to Shaw to keep the Colts undefeated in the seventh week of the season against the Giants in New York. It would be his first start at the quarterback position he once owned two years ago. Shaw threw three touchdown passes, with Moore grabbing two of them among his six receptions, for 181 yards, but it wasn't enough. After a 14–7 halftime lead, the Colts defense broke down. Shaw played brilliantly yet took responsibility for the defeat with a last-minute interception.

"I would have given everything I own to beat the Giants," said a disconsolate Shaw. "The last couple of years sitting on the bench haven't been easy. We are close to a championship now, the first for most of the veterans. All I wanted was to just make a contribution to a victory."

By week's end, Unitas was released from the hospital. Ewbank welcomed him back with open arms and told him that he would accompany the team to Chicago. Ewbank had a hidden reason for it. He had Unitas dress in full uniform, including pads and helmet, as if he were going to play. In the pregame warm-ups, he sent Unitas to midfield so everyone could see that Unitas was ready to play and psychologically do a number on the Bears. All his football life Ewbank would always look for an edge anywhere he could.

Shaw and the rest of the players didn't need any. He, Ameche, and the defense inflicted a 17–0 shutout on the Bears, the first time Chicago had failed to score in 149 games. The defense limited them to 161 yards, Ameche shredded the Bears line for 142 yards in twenty-six carries, and Shaw was ten of twenty-three for 131 yards and a touchdown to Berry.

The Colts returned home to meet the Rams before a throng of 55,557. Unitas started the game with cheers from the large gathering, who were on their feet as he came on the field. On the first snap Unitas took from Nutter, he delivered a 58-yard touchdown pass to Moore, the first of seven Moore would catch, for 162 yards. It was as if Unitas had never missed a game. He was sharp in completing twelve of eighteen passes for 218 yards. Colts fans had their quarterback back. The defense was also glad to see him and showed how much by recovering five fumbles and producing four interceptions as Baltimore was nearing a title at 8–1.

The crowds kept coming, and 57,557 of them couldn't believe what was happening the following week against San Francisco. They sat in disbelief as the 49ers zoomed into a 27–7 first-half bulge and appeared in control of the befuddled Colts.

Baltimore had a disastrous half with only 92 yards of offense compared to the gaudy 231 total compiled by San Francisco. The Colts needed just to come away with a tie to assure themselves of the Western Division crown.

Never in the history of the franchise had the Colts made up 20 points in a half. Y. A. Tittle was playing a flawless game in leading the 49ers on two 80-yard touchdown drives. It was a subdued Colts dressing room. Then Ewbank picked up a piece of chalk and wrote in big letters on the blackboard: "4 TDs." He then turned and looked at his downtrodden players and yelled, "No more 49er points either."

The players responded. The Colts grabbed the second-half kickoff, and Unitas took them on a fifteen-play journey for a touchdown. He did so by changing his strategy to a short passing game, one that the 49ers never adjusted to. When the final quarter began, Unitas was at his best. This time he called for the long ball and delivered a 50-yard pass to Mutscheller to set up Ameche's second touchdown, 27–21, and a winnable situation.

Moore made it happen. He took a handoff, headed for the sidelines, and without losing a step, cut back to the middle of the field and raced 73 yards for the winning touchdown that would give the Colts their first championship. An exhausted Moore was mobbed by his teammates when he reached the Colts bench.

Unitas wasn't through. When the Colts had the ball with some three minutes remaining on their 27, Unitas operated with the precision of a burglar. In eleven plays he got Baltimore another touchdown, completing his cache with a 7-yard toss to Berry. The fans poured out on the field, and Baltimore celebrated.

"When we came back on the field for the second half, we played the greatest half of football I've ever seen," extolled a tired Moore, who congratulated Ameche for the block he made on the 73-yard run. "I saw daylight, and something in my mind kept repeating, "Go, Lenny, go. You got to make it." That's all I wanted to do—to make it. We could have done anything, beaten anybody. This was something magical."

~

The Colts were wired to play for the championship the very next week, but first they had to make their annual West Coast trip to Los Angeles and San Francisco, where they had been victorious only once in eighteen appearances. It didn't matter now. The Western bauble belonged to them. They lost to the Rams, 30–28, and were flat against the 49ers, 16–12.

They wouldn't be flat on December 28.

THE PLAYOFF

Perfection

It would almost be asking too much for the Giants to win another game, even one that meant the Eastern Division championship. They had an innocuous beginning with a listless exhibition campaign and a docile first month of the regular season, winding up nothing better than a .500 club. They lived with adversity all year long when every game they played was one they needed to win. Somehow they managed and never wavered in what was asked of them. And, in the end, they caught Cleveland and forced a playoff.

"We won because we were able to come up with the big play at the right time," emphasized Giants coach Jim Lee Howell. "When a big play was needed on attack, our offense came up with it. And when we needed a big play to stop them, our defense came up with it."

What mattered most to Howell was that his team triumphed when victory was virtually a must. That was never more evident than in the last game against Cleveland. It was the second time they had beaten the Browns, and that alone was a season in itself. The odds were certainly not favorable in beating a team three times in a year, especially a quality one like the Browns. The Giants' inner strength was defense, and their all-too-familiar challenge was Jim Brown. That meant Huff versus Brown, one gladiator against another.

●

Samuel Robert Lee Huff was as country as the hollows in the small mining hamlet of Farmington, West Virginia. He might have remained there if the plane had arrived on time in Burlington, Vermont, his rookie season of 1956. He was only twenty-one, and the rough treatment he experienced, the yelling and the embarrassment, wasn't to his liking. Huff and another rookie, Don Chandler, quickly became homesick and decided to leave. Huff, who had played tackle and linebacker at West Virginia University, had been moved to guard by the Giants and was uncomfortable with the switch.

"You'll never forgive yourself if you leave now," cautioned line coach Ed Kolman. "You'll feel like a quitter."

"It isn't working out, and I'm wasting my time here," disagreed Huff.

"I've seen some great ones," said Kolman. "I think that if you stick it out, you could be one of them in a few years. You've got talent, and I mean it. Don't throw it away by leaving."

"Coach, it's not the football," said Huff. "I can play football. First of all, I'm homesick. And, next, it's Jim Lee Howell. He's on me so much I just can't take it. I really can't. I had pride in my attitude here, so I'm getting out."

Huff and Chandler packed their bags and went to turn in their notebooks a half hour later. They looked for Howell, but he wasn't around, so they woke up Vince Lombardi.

"What the hell do you want?" Lombardi yelled.

"Coach, we quit," answered Huff.

They left behind a cursing, screaming Lombardi. But it wasn't the last they would see of him. Huff and Chandler were waiting in the airport terminal for their late-arriving plane when Lombardi showed up.

"Hold on," ordered Lombardi. "You may not make this club, Chandler, but you're sure as hell not quitting on me now. And neither are you, Huff."

By his own admission, Huff was not very good at guard. He enjoyed playing defense because he liked to hit. Tom Landry, who was putting his four-three defense together, asked Huff if he would mind trying linebacker. The position came naturally to him, and he showed it in the first exhibition game against the Cardinals. It looked as if he had played there his entire career in displaying speed and quickness. He opened the regular season as a $7,000 rookie middle linebacker. Huff had come a long way for a homesick country boy.

"I was brought up in a coal-mining area of West Virginia," related Huff. "We were poor, poor, but I was happy. My father worked in the mines. He didn't make enough money for me to go to college. As a kid, I didn't have but one pair of shoes. I'd go barefoot most of the time, and I couldn't wait for May to come so I could take off my shoes. My mom would slip me twenty-five cents sometimes to go to the movies.

"I lived in what we called a four-room rowhouse, living room, kitchen, and two bedrooms, with a big stove in the middle of the living room. I never had my own room. I shared a bed with my brother. We didn't have any indoor plumbing. We had an outhouse. We'd make our own bread, planted our own garden, and had a big pot of soup for three days. I never dreamed about pro football."

The Giants, after a resilient campaign, were all living the dream now. Huff, the fulcrum of Landry's defense, would have to perform like a bloodhound in tracking Jim Brown's every move to prevent a repeat of the 148 yards he had generated a week earlier. He was groomed by Landry like no other player, and in only his third year of professional football, he had become one of the elite linebackers in the NFL. He never forgot how much Landry did for him in making him a starting linebacker as a rookie. Both lived in the Concourse Plaza Hotel, just a five-minute walk from Yankee Stadium, and they developed a close bond.

"I'd be watching television, and the phone would ring," said Huff. "It was Tom. 'What are you doing?' he'd say, and I'd reply, 'Oh, nothing.' Then he'd say, 'Well, come on up and watch some football with me.' He had this projector in his apartment, and we'd go over the other team's offense. I learned more football in one season in Tom's room than I had learned all through high school and college."

For the last three years under Landry, the defense had become the toughest challenge for their opponents. They had even replaced the traditional heroes on offense as the darlings of the New York crowd. Their success wasn't only the result of brute strength but of a demanding intellectual discipline preached by Landry. To a man, all eleven of them, they were passionately convinced that they could dominate rather than simply contain an opposing team.

"You've got to have experience," said Andy Robustelli. "We've played together, drank together, traveled together, and beefed together. We're close and proud of each other. We know each other so well, we can almost feel each other think."

The Giants were not spectacular on offense because they lacked speed. There were over seventy long scoring plays of 40 yards or more in the NFL during the season, and the Giants could account for only one of them. It was the defense that was their vanguard, and Lou Groza, the Cleveland kicker, who had been around the league a long time, was well aware of it.

"We always respected the Giants' defense," he said. "They have a combination of personnel and basic offenses that are fundamental in theory and solid in performance. We believe they are one of the best defensive teams in the league since they've been in it."

What Cleveland needed besides the magnificence of Jim Brown was just an above-average game from Milt Plum. In two games against the Giants, Plum performed recklessly. He was only four of fourteen in the October game and six of twelve the last week. He was being outplayed by his adversary, Charlie Conerly, who was fifteen years older but didn't show it, being twenty-five of fifty-two. Still, Cleveland coach Paul Brown was thinking about having Plum throw the ball more this time and hinted at that by saying Plum should look at the passing game more openly. Despite two straight losses to the Giants, Brown wasn't concerned about the third challenge.

"I don't believe that morale or mental attitude will be any problem at all," he remarked, still rankled by the Gifford call the week before, which he considered a fumble. "It's one thing I'm not worried about. The guys felt badly about losing, but they know they played a darn fine football game. As a matter of fact, it was one of our best team efforts.

"Deep down, I still think we won. The fellows feel the same way. We know we should have had the football after that fumble. That's part of the game we're in, though, and we accept it, get it out of our minds and go on. Last Sunday we didn't get the break we waited for, but maybe it will come this Sunday. The game takes funny twists."

Jim Lee Howell wasn't expecting anything different from the Browns. He was just thankful that the Giants could play for the championship after being all but counted out. The team had indeed come a long way for the opportunity, and Howell couldn't ask for anything more.

"I don't know what Cleveland will do," admitted Howell, "but I don't think it will depart much from what they tried in the first two games. They used Brown a lot last week, and I expect they will use him a lot again. They always throw to Ray Renfro against us, and they probably will again. One thing that surprised me a little was that they didn't run Lew Carpenter as much as they usually do."

Landry, the choreographer of the Giants defense, agreed.

"They'll try a lot of things, but I doubt if they will throw a lot of passes," concurred Landry. "They may throw a few more than the dozen they did last Sunday."

Lombardi and his offense were looking for an unfrozen field. "A dry field would help us," he pointed out. "Our offense is built more on quick cuts than power."

—

It was another cold December Sunday, yet 61,274 Giants die-hards showed up in 25-degree weather. Before sixty minutes of championship football would evolve, they would sound their battle cry of "Dee-Fense" a hundred times during the epochal contest.

They didn't wait long for the first opportunity. In an unusual move, Jim Brown received the opening kickoff and provided Cleveland with excellent field position on a 41-yard return to the 42. Plum quickly reached New York terrain with a 19-yard completion to Darrel Brewster on the 39. It was a good start for the Browns when the first chant for "Dee-Fense" sounded. All eyes were on Brown. Plum spun and tightly handed him the ball. Jim Katcavage went straight after him and delivered a jarring tackle, one that created a fumble. Rosie Grier, close by, recovered on the 38 to eliminate Cleveland's first threat.

As usual, Don Heinrich started at quarterback. This time he came out throwing instead of probing the Browns defense with running plays. The Giants would have been better doing that. Heinrich's first pass was inaccurate, and his second was inter-cepted by Junior Wren on Cleveland's 42-yard line. The Browns had good field position again. However, Plum was too anxious. He tried to go deep to Carpenter, only to have his pass intercepted by Lindon Crow on the Giants 19.

Heinrich returned for the scripted second time. When Frank Gifford could gather only 2 yards and Alex Webster 3, he was looking for a first down to generate momentum. He needed to throw a pass, especially a safe one. He did exactly that to Webster, who broke loose for 31 yards to the Cleveland 45. Feeling confident, Heinrich then went deep to Gifford but missed. However, Webster ran for 7 and Mel Triplett for 3, and the Giants had another first down on the 35. Heinrich returned to his passing game. He missed with Gifford again and overthrew Kyle Rote. He tried Rote again, this time short, but it was intercepted by linebacker Vince Costello.

Cleveland uncovered another new play for Brown. Taking a lateral from Plum, he faked a run and threw, unfortunately, to a tackle, Mike McCormack, an illegal receiver. It cost the Browns an 8-yard loss on the play along with a 15-yard penalty. Katcavage came through with another big play, spilling Plum for a 5-yard loss that left the Browns on the 15-yard line. Cleveland was precariously close to giving up field position when Plum ran a draw for 16 yards. He then avoided danger by completing a 16-yard throw to Brown. A well-placed punt left the Giants on the 16-yard line and their third possession of the contest.

None other than Conerly made his appearance. He explored the ground route. In two plays, Gifford totaled 7 yards, and Triplett accounted for the first down with an 8-yard pickup. Conerly had some breathing room on the 31, which enabled him to get off a 10-yard pass to Bob Schnelker. When two running plays collected only 4 yards, Conerly took charge and delivered an 11-yard throw to Rote on the Cleveland 44.

The Giants were in sync. After Triplett reached the 42, Webster maneuvered around the left side for 11 yards and another first down on the 31. Conerly tried a pass to Rote that was ineffective. He then called Webster's number for a pass and connected on the 18 for the Giants fifth first down on a balanced controlled drive. He kept Webster involved on a trick play with a handoff. Webster then turned and transferred the ball to Gifford, who gained 8 yards before lateraling to Conerly, whose aging legs carried him to a touchdown. The crowd cheered zealously for old Charlie and the 7–0 lead.

A short kickoff allowed the Browns to begin on their 37. Carpenter could only find a yard before Plum found Brewster with a 29-yard strike on the Giants 33 as the first quarter came to a close. Plum began the second with an 8-yard completion to Carpenter. Katcavage then came up with another big play, chasing Plum out of bounds for a 14-yard loss to the 39. A shook-up Plum was replaced by Jim Ninowski, and a second charge by Katcavage forced him into an inaccurate throw. Groza was asked to kick a 46-yard field goal but missed to the left.

The Giants couldn't advance even a yard and were fortunate that Gifford recovered his own fumble on the 15. It was Chandler who got them out of danger. He boomed a 64-yard punt that rolled dead on the Cleveland 21. Plum tried to get the offense going, but Robustelli put a quick end to any movement. On third down, he tackled Plum for an 11-yard loss, which made the Browns punt. The Giants defense was performing the way Landry groomed them.

Conerly picked up the tempo. He was in concert with Schnelker with a 35-yard pass to the Cleveland 25. With one toss, he had the Giants near field goal territory. Three running plays got them there. Pat Summerall was summoned for a 26-yard field goal attempt. There was only eight minutes remaining in the half when he extended the Giants' advantage to 10–0. For the remainder of the quarter, neither the Giants nor the Browns could produce a first down. When Cleveland had the ball, Crow made a vital play by intercepting Ninowski's long pass on the Giants 5-yard line. Conerly needed to manufacture a first down to run out the clock. He not only got one but he delivered two, the last on a 26-yard gallop by Gifford. It was a perfect half of football. The Browns were limited to only three first downs and 91 yards. Incredibly, Jim Brown had only three carries for a minus 1 yard. Could the defense contain him for the final thirty minutes? Why wasn't he given the ball more? Only three carries? It created conversation in the press box.

The beginning of the second half didn't stir any excitement. New York didn't make a first down, and neither did Cleveland. When the Giants had the ball the second time, they almost scored. Two running first downs brought them to the 42-yard line of Cleveland. Conerly went for the big play and should have produced it. However, his long pass to Gifford, who was wide open, was overthrown. Conerly kicked the ground in disgust.

After one first down, Cleveland went nowhere. The Giants didn't do anything either. As the third quarter was nearing an end, the Browns got two breaks on Giants miscues but couldn't capitalize on either one. Dick Modzelewski nailed Ninowski for an 11-yard loss and forced a punt. However, the sure-handed Em Tunnell dropped the ball, and Jim Shofner retrieved it for the Browns on the Giants 35. Three plays later, Katcavage put on a rush and sacked Plum for a 9-yard loss. The Browns punted again, and once more the Giants fumbled. This time it was Don Maynard, and Gene Hickerson recovered on the Giants 34.

Two shoddy plays brought moans from the crowd and anguish three plays later. Plum got a first down with a pass completion, and Brown followed with a 10-yard run for another on the Giants 4-yard line. The rhythmic chant of "Dee-Fense" filled the air. Cleveland had a fresh set of downs to get 4 yards. Brown got nothing. Plum faded back to pass, and Huff, remembering everything Landry taught him, crashed through unimpeded and toppled him for a 12-yard loss to the 16 as the crowd cheered loudly at the third-quarter's end.

On third down, Plum faked a handoff to Brown and set up to pass. Huff, without having to worry about Brown, dropped back in coverage. He read Plum's eyes and coolly intercepted him on the 5-yard line to end Cleveland's twelve-play drive. It was a huge interception, and Plum walked to the sidelines with his head down. The Giants didn't have to take any unnecessary chances now. They worked on the clock with six running plays before Chandler got off a 54-yard punt.

The strong-armed Ninowski took over for Plum and immediately began throwing. He hit Brewster for 8 yards and Carpenter for 6 and a first down on the 37. That was as far as he got. Harland Svare broke up his next pass and Tunnell the next one. When Ninowski missed with his third one, the Browns had to punt.

Time became the Giants' ally. Each play now would become a clock killer. They took their time in the huddle and began on the 34 with their obvious ground game. After a 2-yard gain by Gifford, the Giants found themselves in trouble when an in-motion penalty pushed them back 5 yards, and Phil King was corralled for a 5-yard loss. On third down, the Giants needed 18 yards to maintain possession.

Cleveland defended for the pass, but Conerly outsmarted them. He wanted Gifford on a reverse, and the play was perfectly executed for 19 yards. A loud ovation vibrated from the stands, and the Giants defense pumped their arms skyward in celebration. The Giants were a precious six minutes away from wearing the Eastern Division crown.

Conerly took it from there. He decided that all he would do would be to hand the ball to his running backs. Webster, Gifford, Triplett, and King kept coming at the Browns and pounded their way for three first downs. On the thirteenth running play, in what must have seemed an eternity to the Browns, the Giants finally yielded the ball on the Cleveland 26. The Giants drive was so effective and so time consuming that the Browns had only one harmless play left. An incomplete pass sealed the Giants' magnificent playoff success.

The Giants defense totally dominated the Browns. It was their finest performance, in every sense a perfect game. Cleveland only gained a total of 86 yards, which paled to New York's 317. Only seven times the Browns moved the first-down chains, while the Giants did it on seventeen occasions. Landry's defense, led by Sam Huff, removed Jim Brown from the game. He gained only 8 yards the seven times he carried the ball. Brown and the Browns were subjugated like never before almost to the point of ridicule.

"This is the best defensive effort against a top team that I've ever seen in pro football," crowed Jim Lee Howell. "And that goes for the 1950 Giants and any other team of the past. They had fire and determination today. Sam Huff and Jim Katcavage are youngsters who just don't know how to lose. And Andy Robustelli is a great money player. Everyone on that defensive team did a wonderful job."

Then he looked over at Landry.

"I'm not just passing around bouquets," he continued. "Tom has been in complete charge. That's the way we work things here. He's the greatest defensive coach I've ever seen. You take Paul Brown three times, and you've done something."

Brown was somber yet professional in a subdued Cleveland dressing room, exasperated in losing three times to the Giants, and this one, the last one, the most galling one.

"We were soundly defeated," admitted Brown humbly. "New York's defensive team overpowered our offense. It was an inspired team in front of a wild, rooting home audience. We had trouble throwing, and they made great catches. They outplayed us. Our defensive team played a fine game. Any time a team is held to 10 points it should be enough to win in this league. The Giants are a very fine team, and they are from our division, so we wish them well against the Colts."

It was Frank Gifford who was the game's top rusher, not the renowned Jim Brown, with 95 yards. He was also directly responsible for the game's only touchdown, the one by Charlie Conerly, which came as a surprise to the craggy quarterback.

"It was a reverse to me from Webster," explained Gifford. "Lombardi had designed the play to take advantage of the Browns' strong pursuit, and it worked perfectly. As I reached the Browns 8, I knew I could take it in. But out of the corner of my eye, I saw my thirty-seven-year-old buddy wheezing along behind me.

"I just couldn't resist the temptation, so I flipped him a quick lateral. Charlie was totally stunned. There was a look of stark terror in his eyes. But he caught the ball and just made it to the end zone. On the way back to the bench, Charlie muttered to me between gasps, 'Next time I give you the fucking ball, you keep it.'"

Howell relished the play. "They kidded around with it at practice last week, but I didn't think they'd call it," he said. "We've used the double reverse before, but the lateral to Conerly was a new wrinkle. Hey, I'm scared to death of the Colts."

Herb Levy, a rabid Giants fan from Brooklyn, will always remember the game, but not for the usual reason. Levy was being discharged from the Army that weekend in Houston and was looking forward to a double celebration in New York, a Giants victory and getting formally engaged to Adrienne Lankin from Detroit. He and his father planned on attending the game followed by a family dinner, at which time he would surprise Adrienne with an engagement ring.

Unfortunately, it didn't unfold the way Herb had intended. He was grounded by an airplane strike that Saturday and scrambled to secure a train connection that would get him to New York by Sunday morning. However, the only ticket he could purchase wasn't a direct one. He caught a local that went north to St. Louis before heading east. Train delays derailed him from getting to the game on time.

His family had planned to be at Grand Central Terminal when he arrived. But in another quirk on the arduous journey, the train was diverted to Pennsylvania Station, which was on the west side of the city. By six o'clock, Adrienne finally got her ring and the celebration that accompanied it.

The Giants did their celebrating at Toots Shor's. Where else?

GAME DAY

Thirteen Plays to Glory

When the Colts arrived in New York late Saturday morning, December 27, there were no newspapers heralding their arrival. The city was experiencing the effrontery of an eighteen-day strike that paralyzed all seven of the daily chronicles. Weeb Ewbank encountered an inconvenience with the strike. He was a strong advocate of bulletin board fodder and delighted in tacking articles on the clubhouse wall that degraded his team. Friends in the cities that the Colts appeared would send Ewbank any such derogatory stories, and he would derive satisfaction in posting them himself for all of his players to read. As far as Weeb was concerned, the articles were more effective than Knute Rockne's fabled "win one for the Gipper" speech. However, the players didn't take it seriously and often joked about the items.

It certainly wasn't the best of times to be in New York, with a lingering number of tourists still around celebrating the Christmas season with no periodicals to guide them. The Broadway theater district felt the effect of the strike the most. Seven new shows had opened, three of which were forced to close, while the rest struggled to make their arrival known. It also meant the ticket brokers couldn't command a princely sum for first-nighters seeking entertainment.

Of the twenty-seven shows lighting up Broadway, only *The Flower Drum Song, My Fair Lady, The Music Man, Hamlet, The World of Suzie Wong, La Plume de Ma Tante,* and *The Marriage-Go-Round* reported sellouts or near-capacity audiences. A number of shows expressed fears that they would have to close down if the strike lasted another week. *Variety,* the clarion of the entertainment world, succinctly summed up the theater crisis with the catchy headline "B'way Blitzed." But at least Wall Streeters found joy. A seat on the New York Stock Exchange was sold that week for $135,000, which was $2,000 more than the previous price.

The game was a bane to New Yorkers. It was blacked out on television, and no one could read about it because of the lingering newspaper strike. Yet there were some television owners who were fortunate in that they could watch the event. Because of the vagaries of television waves, city dwellers who lived north of the Empire State Building were able to pick up the signal from a Philadelphia station, some 90 miles south. To those opportune viewers, Philadelphia was indeed every bit the City of Brotherly Love.

Ewbank was looking for an edge and any information he could extract. He learned that from his years as an assistant coach under Paul Brown, who had the highest winning percentage of any professional coach. Brown, too, was resolvent in anything he did.

Ewbank was cautioned by Brown at a draft meeting in Philadelphia one year not to even put his briefcase on the floor while registering for a room because before he could finish signing his name, the case would disappear. They weren't the only ones looking for an edge.

It was in Cleveland where Ewbank developed his paranoia. During the Colts practices, he would have someone check on anybody he didn't recognize, and none of the maintenance workers were exempt. That's how paranoid he was.

Ewbank decided to employ his own form of espionage in the person of Bob Shaw, an assistant coach who also scouted opponents. Even though the Colts had already played the Giants three times, twice in the exhibition season and once in the regular campaign, he nevertheless chose to dispatch Shaw to New York to secretly attend one of the Giants practices in Yankee Stadium. It was a common procedure a number of teams would employ, but not with a scout, and getting inside Yankee Stadium was practically the equivalent of entering Fort Knox unannounced. Owner Carroll Rosenbloom was so obsessed with winning the title that he encouraged Shaw to fulfill his spy mission. But Shaw wasn't so confident.

"What if they catch me?" he asked.

"Don't let that worry you," assured Rosenbloom. "If anything like that occurs, you have a job with me in any of my companies for life."

Shaw left for New York with the security of Rosenbloom's lifetime promise. Appearing incognito as much as possible, with his head down and his overcoat collar turned up, he circled Yankee Stadium like a homing pigeon. He was looking for an open door, fully cognizant that he would be discovered if he used the players' entrance.

Not finding any, the resourceful Shaw crossed the street behind centerfield, entered a tall apartment building, and took the elevator to the top floor. He walked up a flight of stairs, opened the door to the roof, and looked down on a panoramic view of the stadium. Peering through his binoculars, he detected the Giants running a double halfback reverse that Shaw hadn't seen before in the earlier games against the Giants. Shaw gleefully returned to Baltimore and delivered the information to the megalomaniac Ewbank.

The Giants, who had won the NFL championship in 1956, were primed to make it two of the last three years. So what if the Colts had won nine of their last ten games, while the Giants needed to win a playoff game to make it to the championship? They had painted a Rembrandt in winning the East. Not only did they shut out Cleveland, 10–0, but they stuffed Jim Brown, the game's greatest running back, limiting him to only 8 yards on seven carries. Nobody had ever done that before.

The reason was Sam Huff, the linchpin of a smart Giants defense and why they reached the championship game. Like a sheriff, he followed Brown's every move, even when he didn't have the ball, and gunned him down before he could use his moves and his power to outrun the posse. Huff had joined the Giants in 1956, the same year Johnny Unitas came to Baltimore as a free agent. Huff had already made a name for himself with his stalking play and was the most revered member of the Giants defense. Unitas was still waiting to make his mark, and when the long afternoon of gut football was finally over, he would.

—

There was no argument that the Colts and the Giants were the two best teams in 1958, and whoever emerged victorious would be genuine champions. Baltimore's offense was awesome, averaging 31.8 points a game. Their defense was substantial but never achieved the acclaim the offense did. Not so for the Giants. Defense was their forte, magnified in the playoff game, which was the second time it produced a shutout in holding opponents to 16.5 points a game. Offense against defense: It couldn't get better than that if a script had to be written, and what better place than New York for a Cinderella Baltimore quarterback?

Nobody in the crowd of 64,185 who made their way into Yankee Stadium that Sunday, or the million or so who were watching a championship game on television for the first time, would sense that they would become observers to history. The nation was in the grips of a recession, fans of the Dodgers and Giants were still mourning the loss of their baseball teams to Los Angeles and San Francisco, and twenty-three-year-old rock 'n' roll heartthrob Elvis Presley was picking up Army boots that morning in Nashville. But nothing that day for the fans in Yankee Stadium was bigger than the Colts and the Giants playing for the NFL championship.

Colts fans rendered testimony to that. All 15,000 game tickets that were allotted to the Baltimore club were sold out overnight. Most of them traveled by train well equipped with winter gear to fortify themselves against the anticipated cold of a New York December. As the train traveled north and through the flatlands of New Jersey, they were a joyful bunch. It was their biggest game ever, too. And when Sunday arrived, New York cooperated with a mild afternoon greeting of 49 degrees. "Rosenbloom Weather," they called it.

Yankee Stadium was an intimidating venue. It was hallowed ground, and the Yankees won more championships than anybody in baseball. Ruth, Gehrig, DiMaggio, and now Mantle were the symbols of Yankee glory, and their craftsmanship was deeply embedded in baseball lore. That was the dogma the Colts had to exorcise before they even stepped on the field. Art Donovan knew about it. He grew up within a stone's throw of the triple-decked edifice. His father, Arthur Sr., had refereed championship fights at the stadium, and as a kid he was there to inhale and savor the golden moments.

It was a humbling setting for a Colts team that had no lore of their own. They were vagabonds who only knew survival. And survive they did to the biggest game in their history. Munificently, they were established as 3-point favorites. The difference, the oddsmakers felt, was Unitas. On this day, he would be every inch a gladiator. Before he would leave the dressing room, he had to be dressed with 9 pounds of padding around his chest to protect three broken ribs that were tender since the fourth game of the season, along with a punctured lung that required hospitalization.

Nobody had known anything about Unitas when he joined the Colts off the grimy Pittsburgh sandlots. He was by and large a blank, and here he was in the biggest game of his life at the age of twenty-four. Ewbank, who had a penetrating eye for talent, had seen something in the skinny kid and got him a contract. Yet Ewbank never so much as fantasized that Unitas would matriculate so quickly and would be his quarterback in a championship game.

Neither did the Giants, or anyone else for that matter. Unitas's quantum leap was reflected in an exhibition game his rookie year. The Giants were playing a night game against the Colts in Boston, leading late in the fourth quarter, when Unitas entered the contest. Charlie Conerly, who was standing next to Frank Gifford, wasn't impressed with his first look at Unitas.

"Look at that goofy son-of-a-bitch," observed Conerly.

In their eyes, Unitas was gangly, hunched over, and definitely pigeon-toed. If he had appeared on a quiz show, no one would take him for a professional football player, not with rubber bands holding up his sleeves. Instead of running out the clock, though, Unitas began throwing. He was trying to pull out the game, make an impression, and win a spot on the roster, which irked both Gifford and Conerly. They wanted to catch a plane back to New York and make it to Shor's or P. J. Clarke's.

"Who is that guy?" asked Gifford.

Conerly turned, walked over to the bench, and came back a minute later.

"U-na-tis," drawled Conerly.

"Sounds like a Greek drugstore chain," remarked Gifford.

The Colts' date with destiny began on the Saturday morning before the game, in Baltimore. Their United Airlines charter left Friendly Airport at ten o'clock. The players were informed that no breakfast would be served on the flight. Instead, coffee, milk, and sweet rolls would be available, which, for football players, wasn't hardly breakfast but a snack, if that. Anyway, breakfast wasn't on the players' minds, so no one complained. The flight time to New York's LaGuardia Airport

```
ITINERARY FOR CHAMPIONSHIP GAME IN NEW YORK, DECEMBER 28, 1958

                         Saturday, December 27

    9:15 AM   EST    Report Baltimore Friendship Airport.

   10:00 AM   EST    Depart Baltimore for New York via United
                     Airlines Charter.

   11:10 AM   EST    Arrive New York - LaGuardia Airport.  Campus Coach
                     Buses to Concourse Plaza Hotel.

    1:15 PM   EST    Depart for practice at Yankee Stadium.

    4:30 PM   EST    Dinner at Concourse Plaza Hotel.  Announcements.

    6:30 PM   EST    Team meeting.

    9:30 PM   EST    Snack at Concourse Plaza Hotel.

   10:00 PM   EST    Room check.

                         Sunday, December 28

   10:00 AM   EST    Pre-game meal at Concourse Plaza Hotel.

                     Consult taping schedule.

   12:30 PM   EST    Depart Concourse Plaza Hotel for Yankee Stadium
                     via Campus Coach Buses.

    2:05 PM   EST    Kickoff - Colts vs. New York Giants.

                     Depart Yankee Stadium for LaGuardia Airport via
                     Campus Coach Line Buses following the game.

    6:30 PM   EST    Depart New York LaGuardia Airport for Baltimore
                     via United Airlines Charter.  Dinner to be served
                     on plane.

    7:40 PM   EST    Arrive Baltimore Friendship Airport.


              *       *       *       *


Note:  No breakfast will be served on Saturday morning flight -
       coffee, milk and sweet rolls will be available.
```

This schedule for the championship weekend was given to the Colts players. **Courtesy Pro Football Hall of Fame** would take a little over an hour, leaving the players ample time for the scheduled 1:15 p.m. workout at Yankee Stadium. For the most part, the players' mood was quiet, almost subdued, much like the coaches' disposition in the front rows of the aircraft. United and Unitas. There had to be something to that. An omen perhaps.

Baltimore's contingent was billeted at the Concourse Plaza Hotel, which was across the street from the Bronx County Courthouse. Several long Unitas passes away was majestic Yankee Stadium. Art Donovan, the burly veteran defensive tackle, knew the neighborhood. He was a Bronx boy who played his high school football at Mt. St. Michael before getting a scholarship to Boston College. As a mischievous kid, he used to steal beers with several of his buddies from the Saturday night dances at the Plaza. Donovan, too, was looking for respect, and his was personal.

"Before this game, I could be standing outside Mr. Goldberg's candy store, and he'd see me and say, 'Donovan, you big bum, are you out of work again?' laughed Donovan. "He had no idea that I played football. The league, it was in its infancy then."

After a 4:30 p.m. dinner, the players gathered in the team meeting room at 6:30 to discuss the key elements of strategy they would employ the next day. They were very well versed about the solid Giants defense, Huff in particular, and needed to construct a way to limit his effectiveness. The offensive game plan was to keep good splits along the line, which would benefit the Colts running game and provide pass protection for Unitas. The ends and the flanking backs were instructed to keep as wide as possible in order to open the passing lanes.

Regarding the oppressive Huff, the coaches felt that it should be easier to run away from him if he didn't stay in the middle of the Giants four-three defense. They noted that his tendency was to follow the fullback most of the time and that a draw play and inside runs would be effective. To set the offense in gear, Unitas was urged to go on quick counts to discourage defensive moving, especially the blitz. By ten o'clock, the players were in their rooms. There were no wives this time. Ewbank was convinced that the Colts had lost to the Giants in the second week of the season because the wives were around. None of the players bought into that. They felt they lost because Unitas was in the hospital having blood drawn from a punctured lung and couldn't play.

Donovan was one of the first to awaken on Sunday morning. By 7:15 a.m. he was on his way to church with Bert Rechichar, a defensive back who handled the kickoffs, and Jack Call, a reserve halfback. They had ample time for Mass but not enough time for Donovan to visit his parents' apartment forty blocks away. That would have to wait until his next visit, when he would also make a stop at Goldberg's candy store.

The team's pregame meal wasn't until ten o'clock, and the chartered bus for the short ride to the stadium was at 12:30. Heck, Donovan would have walked there if they'd let him. He was home alright, extolling the beauty of the Bronx and his childhood mischief to anyone who would listen. At thirty, he was the oldest Colts in point of service on the team, and he earned that respect regardless of all his boisterous moments in chiding his teammates.

Some of the Colts got their first look at Sam Huff at the hotel that morning. He lived there during the season and was in the coffee shop having breakfast. None of the Colts players said anything to him. After all, he was a hated enemy, one whose picture would appear on the cover of *Time* magazine a year later and be immortalized the following year in a CBS documentary,

The Violent World of Sam Huff, narrated by Walter Cronkite. However, one of the Baltimore writers somehow started a conversation with Huff, who already had on his game face. He jokingly suggested to the extraordinary linebacker that he had time to catch the one o'clock train to West Virginia.

Huff looked straight at him.

"I can always take the train to West Virginia, but I can't always go out and win the world championship," he snarled, then got up and left.

L. G. Dupre and Ray Berry were the only Colts who didn't appear at the pregame meal, but they had reason not to. They never liked eating a big meal before a game, championship or otherwise, and they received permission to eat in the coffee shop, where they settled for scrambled eggs. Being a Bible-toting practitioner, Berry preferred the solitude anyway. Before this day would end, he would make believers of anyone who saw him play.

The taping in room 626 had its humorous moments. Naturally, Donovan provided most of it. He had a small hole in his undershorts when he entered the room that trainer Dick Spassoff had arranged to tape the players' ankles and whatever else they needed medically. It wasn't a large room, and the players entered in groups of four until all thirty-three of them were attended to. Donovan, being the jokester he was, got them laughing.

"I feel like I'm going to be so rich today, and here's what I'm going to do," he shouted.

At that moment he looked down, took one of his meaty fingers, placed it in the torn spot, and in one quick motion ripped the pants off his big body. The room howled with laughter. Dupre then added to it while having his ankles taped. Like a racehorse, Dupre could run, and his initials L. G. translated to his nickname, "Long Gone."

"Nobody likes your tape job, Spassoff, but I do," exclaimed Dupre.

"My little sweater boy," said Spassoff, smiling. "I will give you a two-touchdown tape job."

The taping session was almost over, and Jim Parker, the team's outstanding 270-pound tackle, wished it would have happened sooner. He came crashing down to the floor when all four legs of the chair he was sitting on gave way all at once. Parker came down with a thud, but, fortunately, he wasn't hurt. Laughter again resonated in the room as Spassoff picked up the remaining parts of the broken chair. He wasn't troubled by it at all. "We're going to win, we're going to win," he shouted.

Buzz Nutter, Unitas's certitude center, wondered out loud about who won last week's game. That, too, contributed to some laughs. "Who won that game between the Browns and the Giants last week?" he joked. "All that stuff Weeb put us through, and he forgot to tell us who we were going to play."

At exactly 12:30 p.m., as scheduled, the Colts bus made its way to Yankee Stadium. It didn't take long. Before the players could stretch out and get comfortable, they were ready to get off the bus.

"Hey, Horse, how would you like to play two out of three for the title?" asked Carl Taseff, who carried the nickname of Gaucho.

"You know, Gaucho, I think that's a splendid idea," said Alan Ameche. "I could buy that."

Some of the early-arriving Giants fans, what the hell, it was a warm day, stood and watched the intruders from Baltimore. And they had something to say. One recognized Donovan. He was an easy victim. "Hey, Donovan, I hope this team is better than the one you played on at Mount St. Michael's," he teased. Donovan was laughing too hard to answer, one of the few times he was without words. The good-natured heckler must have been from Donovan's neighborhood.

Once inside the locker room, the Colts found no relief. Ewbank himself was particularly out of character in addressing his players after they had finished their pregame warm-ups. Usually a mild-mannered individual, Ewbank was visceral in exhorting the team, calling them out individually by name, and created an eerie silence that froze the players. He began by telling them they all had something to prove, and the place to do it was New York. But then he jolted them by shouting that they were all a bunch of rejects and started blasting away.

"In fourteen years, I heard 'em all," remarked Gino Marchetti. "Win one for Mother. Win for Father. Don't disappoint all these people watching on television. Weeb really put it to us. He went down the roster name by name. 'Ameche, Green Bay didn't want you. . . . Lipscomb, you were released. . . . Berry, people said you'd never be a pro. . . . Donovan, they got rid of you, too fat and slow.'"

Ewbank saved the last for himself. He told his players that he had been the second choice when he was named coach in 1954. Rosenbloom and Don Kellett wanted the other Browns assistant, Blanton Collier. The two even flirted with Buddy Parker and Joe Khuharich and as far away as Iowa's head coach, Forrest Evasheski, to replace Ewbank. In essence, Ewbank personalized the pregame meeting by including himself with the players.

Weeb didn't know it, but Donovan never heard him. He was in the bathroom throwing up when Rechichar, who was in Weeb's doghouse, sauntered in. Rechichar didn't even know if he was going to play or not and couldn't understand why Ewbank was mad at him. Later he got a reprieve when he learned he would kick off.

The world championship game had a unique story line associated with it, simply the haves against the have-nots. It was blue-collar Baltimore against the Madison Avenue Giants. The glamour that personified the New York team was its defense. The manner in which they humbled Jim Brown the week before: What chance could Ameche and Moore have? It was all up to Unitas, and he would devour the challenge. There wasn't any more time to listen to provocations. He had a destiny to fulfill. The daunting nature of the Giants defense presented a quintessential task, and Unitas would have a mild winter day to get it done.

While Baltimore was looking for respect, they were facing a Giants team that already had it, appearing in a championship game for the tenth time. Baltimore, well, no one took them too seriously; they were favored by the oddsmakers, but they lost their final two games of the season and that wasn't looked upon as the best way to play for a championship. But the Colts were described as something different, something no one could explain except as being a lunch pail team who came to play, as evidenced by winning nine of their first ten games with an explosive offense led by Unitas.

There was a great deal more to the Giants defense than Sam Huff. There was Andy Robustelli, a smart, quick defensive stalwart, on one end and rugged Jim Katcavage on the other. The sentinels in the middle of the line were Rosey Grier and oppressive Dick Modzelewski. Unitas was told to throw over Modzelewski, who was 5 inches shorter than Grier. Emlen Tunnell and Jimmy Patton, who had eleven interceptions at the other safety spot, buoyed the defensive backfield.

But on this day there was concern. The Giants were a battered team, and most of them could barely walk through practice during the week. Conerly never appeared on the practice field. The extra playoff game against Cleveland took its toll. The first line of defense, Robustelli, Grier, Modzelewski, and Kat-cavage, were hurting, with Grier's leg the biggest worry.

Defensively, the Giants had limited their opponents to a league-low 183 points during the 1958 season. They won their final four games by yielding a total of 37 points, an average of 9 points a contest. The adage that defense wins games was never more evident than the final month of the Giants' regular season.

The Giants defense was so emblematic that even Cliff Liv-ingston, a less-heralded linebacker, had a television commercial on the local channels. Less imposing was the offense. It relied on the big-play strike rather than the smooth, efficient offense of Baltimore that was the most prolific in the league. There were times during the season where the Giants offense was so lethargic it created concern and would need the yeoman effort of the defense to position touchdowns.

"It got pretty bad," admitted Rote. "I remember once going out to take over on offense after the defense had scored against the Cardinals. Robustelli was coming off, and he stopped to pat me on the back. "See if you can hold them," he remarked.

Baltimore's defense was devoid of the press clippings the Giants had accumulated. They were basically overlooked. But they were a solid outfit in the esteem of the oddsmakers and why they established the Colts as favorites even though they would play on the Giants' home turf. They led the NFL with an alarming thirty-five interceptions, which averaged out to just about three a game.

Unitas's adversary at quarterback, Charlie Conerly, had a bittersweet relationship with Giants fans. When the Giants won, they loved him. When they lost, he was scorned. Conerly, however, had the respect of his teammates and was also a Mara favorite. He wasn't anywhere near the passer the younger Uni-tas was, but he knew how to win on guile and grit. He won some meaningful games with the Giants in the eleven years he'd been with them. In the 47-7 rout of the Bears in the 1956 championship game, which gave the Giants their first title in eighteen years, Conerly threw for two touchdowns.

His craggy looks were special, so much so that he was the original Marlboro Man, which explained why he always had a cigarette close by. Although never a cowboy, he could easily portray one in western movies and did manage to appear in one. This was the veteran Conerly's biggest game of his career, and in movie circles it could be written as the last gunfight at the Yankee corral, with the edge belonging to Unitas.

Conerly was adept at getting the ball to Gifford on a delay coming out of the backfield, an integral part of whatever offense the Giants manufactured. Gifford was the single-biggest threat that the Colts defense had to concern itself with. He led the Giants in rushing, pass receiving, and scoring and could also throw the football. He was cherished by Mara, and Gifford's movie star looks weren't overlooked by the ladies and Madison Avenue. He was a matinee idol.

Gifford and Conerly, both friendly with each other, were the odd couple. Gifford was outward and smiling, while Conerly was tacit and subdued. Yet they hung out together at Toots Shor's and P. J. Clarke's. More often than not, they would be joined by Webster, Summerall, and Rote, the team's offensive hierarchy. Even then, Charlie wouldn't have much to say. He enjoyed the camaraderie, and no one told him that he shouldn't smoke too much. It wasn't that Conerly did the town every night. Quite the contrary; he preferred the quiet apartment hours with his wife, Periann.

"We didn't socialize much," admitted Conerly, "and never before such a big game as this one. I never talked a whole lot to anybody. In the bad years, the booing never bothered me. At the games, heck, that was alright, but not walking down the streets, not in restaurants. I didn't want my wife to put up with that, so we didn't go out much."

Gifford was the catalyst of the offense. He was a multiple-threat performer who could throw a pass, even catch one, and run with deceptive speed with the grace of Joe DiMaggio. He appeared to perfect the art of acrobatic receptions and was a legitimate triple threat. He would perform in this defining game slightly disadvantaged with sore ribs and a bursa sac elbow the size of a tennis ball. The Colts knew his value.

"We were told to key on Frank," disclosed Marchetti. "We were told to follow him wherever he went, to come up fast and never lose sight of him when a play began to develop. There were a hundred ways Frank could beat you."

❧

Unitas was hoping the Colts would win the coin toss when he led two of his teammates to midfield to meet Conerly and two other Giants. The Colts quarterback was primed and anxious to take the first snap from Nutter and lead them downfield for a touchdown. It would send the Giants defense a message that they were not impregnable despite their hyped reputation. But it wasn't to be. The hometown Giants won the coin flip, and they chose to go on offense first instead of conceding to their defense. Rechichar, who was worried if he would get to play, was the first to touch the ball, when his booming kick, accompanied by the crowd's roar, was downed by Don Maynard in the end zone.

Conerly didn't join the Giants in the huddle. Don Heinrich did instead. Coach Jim Lee Howell had been opening games with a series or two with Heinrich before turning to Conerly. His theory was that, by doing this, he and his coaching staff could observe what the opposing team was doing on defense, especially with its blitzing schemes. That was corroborated by

Polaroid film sent down from the press box to the playing field by, of all people, Wellington Mara himself. Conerly didn't share Howell's strategy of starting the game with Heinrich before he took over.

What the Colts defense saw was somewhat surprising. Heinrich normally would call some running plays to feel out the defense. However, in his opening series, he surprised the Colts but didn't fool them, in throwing the ball three straight times. His first pass to Rote was swatted away by a charging

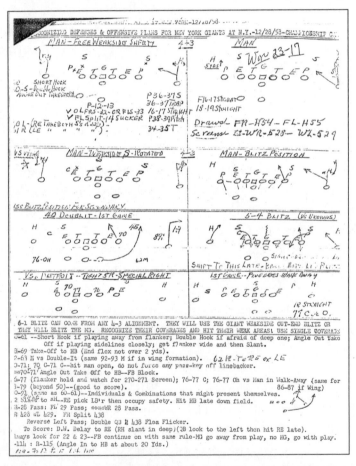

The Colts received this game plan to help them recognize the Giants defensive and offensive schemes. **Courtesy Pro Football Hall of Fame**

Marchetti. Heinrich's next pass was a flare to Alex Webster that netted 7 yards. However, when he tried for a first down to Rote, defensive back Carl Taseff denied it. No one could remember the Giants beginning a game with three consecutive passes.

The Giants defense now had to brace for Unitas. He trotted for the first time to the Colts 30-yard line and huddled his offense. Would he open with a quick pass to Berry or a long one to Moore? Close to 15,000 Colts fans were looking for the bomb in Unitas's arsenal. Instead, Unitas handed off to Moore on a sweep and was dumped for a 3-yard loss by Carl Karilivacz. Unitas was expected to throw in his area throughout the game. Ameche got back some of the lost yardage when he churned inside for 7 yards. On third down, needing 6 yards for a first, Huff summarized a pass. He was right. He shot by Nutter on a blitz, slamming into Unitas hard enough to jar the ball loose from his hands. An opportunistic Patton recovered the ball on the Colts 37.

It was an unlikely start for Unitas. The menacing Huff had given the Giants a propitious opportunity in the opening minutes. The excellent field position should enable the Giants to score first. Sensing that, the partisan crowd roared approvingly as Heinrich reemerged on the field. If he couldn't deliver a touchdown with a stronger arm than Conerly, there was always the reliable Pat Summerall. But Marchetti, a marvelous defensive end, wouldn't allow it. After Webster lost a yard, he burst into the Giants backfield unimpeded, crushed Heinrich, then recovered the quarterback's fumble.

Unitas was only 5 yards from midfield when he appeared on the field a second time. He got there with two plays to Dupre. One was a 4-yard flare pass and the other a 1-yard run. Unitas was looking for a first down and looking for Berry. The hitch pattern dispatched Berry to the Giants 40-yard line, but the reliable receiver never got the ball. Defensive back Lindon Crow recognized the pattern and brought back an interception 5 yards to the 45.

This couldn't be Unitas. A fumble and an interception in his first two series: Was the Giants defense intimidating him? The vaunted Colts offense was limited to just 9 yards.

There were some quizzical expressions in the press box when Heinrich came back for a third time. Where was Conerly? Was he aching too much to play? He was the constant all season long. But now? Surely Gifford, who lost a yard from the Giants 45-yard line, missed him. Mel Triplett tried on the next play but was stopped for no gain. If Howell wanted the strong-armed Heinrich, what was the logic behind two running plays? On third down, Heinrich finally threw. But it was a short pass to Triplett that could only secure 6 yards. Don Chandler had to punt and booted a beauty to the Colts 8-yard line, where Taseff returned it to the 15.

Unitas wasn't one to look back. Never was. He returned for the third time in the shadow of his own goal posts, a poor location to throw from. So, the Giants played to run. But Unitas being Unitas, the master of the unexpected, called Moore's number for a pass. It wasn't a quick pop, a safe pass. It was a long one that would enable Moore's speed to carry him past a defender. Still, Unitas would require enough time to set up and throw for such an audacious circumvention. What if the resourceful Huff broke through and caused him to fumble again? But Baltimore's linemen executed their blocks, which allowed Unitas to firmly grip the ball and wait for Moore to get open. Parker ensured it by taking care of Robustelli. When the moment came, Moore reached up and united with a perfect trajectory of a thrown ball on the Giants 25-yard line, where he was pulled down by Patton. The 60-yard launch brought the crowd to its feet and a pained look on the Giants defenders. Even Giants fans had to marvel at the throw.

With one magnificent pass, the Colts were deep in Giants terrain, in field goal range. Ameche got them closer with a 5-yard run. Dupre tried to negotiate a run-around left end, but it was swarmed over for a loss of a yard. An unlikely delay of game penalty set the Colts back 5 yards to the 21. Moore tried the right side but could only find 2 yards.

The Colts adjusted for a field goal. Steve Myhra, who wasn't anywhere as accurate as Summerall, had made only four of twelve attempts during the season. True to form, he missed from the 24-yard line when his kick sailed wide. Yet the gods smiled on him and gave him another chance when the Giants were penalized for being offsides. Myhra was 5 yards closer and measured his kick from the 19. He never got the opportunity to look up when he kicked. It was the irrepressible Huff again. He rushed straight over center and blocked the frustrated Myhra's practically, certain even for him, 3 pointer.

Donovan looked on with disgust. "Weeb never liked Myhra," intoned Donovan. "His father gave him a million dollars, and he blew it all."

Howell had enough of Heinrich. He sent Conerly into battle, and the veteran quarterback heard cheers when the fans recognized his number 42 jersey. Conerly brought the offense to life after Webster could only get back to the line of scrimmage. A flare pass to Triplett gained 9 yards to the 31. It was Gifford's turn, needing only a yard for a first down. But he got more, much more. He started left. Brown gave him a block, and so did Rote, allowing the Giants' golden boy to roam for 38 yards before he was wrestled down on Baltimore's 31. After Triplett fought for 2 yards, Conerly went to the air. His first pass to Rote fell incomplete, and Webster slipped and fell without catching the ball on the next one. Summerall, the hero of the last two wins over the Browns, trotted onto the field, warmed by the cheers of the crowd. He surveyed a 36-yard field goal challenge and kicked it accurately, giving the Giants a 3–0 lead two minutes from the end of the first quarter.

The high-scoring Colts hadn't scored yet, and there were only 120 seconds left when Unitas lined them up from the 21. Once again the Giants defense frustrated him. He achieved 5 yards on a pass to Moore. Dupre's 3-yard run gave the Colts an opportunity for a first down, but Unitas missed on a pass to Moore as the opening quarter came to a close.

Conerly turned to his pal, Gifford, on the first play of the second quarter. It was a sideline pass that was caught, but Frank, looking ahead at his blockers, fumbled as little-known tackle Ray Krouse recovered for the Colts on the 20.

Unitas had to deliver, not only for his own psyche, but for the rest of the team's as well. Yet Unitas thrived on such challenges, and he was prepared, not only with his deadly passing arm, but with his ground forces. Moore collected 4 yards and Ameche 5. On a big third-down play from the 11, Ameche delivered a precious first down. Moore shook loose to the 2-yard line, and on the next play, Ameche scored the Colts first touchdown. Myhra's conversion made it 7–3. The joy on the sideline was an indication that the Colts scoring machine was primed for more.

Following the kickoff, Conerly set up on the 33, which was decent field position. A Triplett run netted only a yard. Conerly got Giants fans excited with a 14-yard completion to Rote. It quickly turned to anguish when Marchetti and Donovan sandwiched Conerly for a 9-yard loss. On a double reverse from Gifford, Webster could only get 4 yards, and when Conerly missed with a pass to Gifford, the Giants had to punt.

Rookie halfback Jackie Simpson was in position to gather Chandler's punt on the 10-yard line when he fumbled. It could have been attributable to the raucous crowd in the biggest game the kid had ever played in. He dropped the ball without ever being hit, and the Giants recovered right where Simpson dropped it.

The joy on the Colts bench only minutes before was instantly subdued. The Giants were only 10 yards away from retaking the lead. However, no sooner did the defensive unit assume its alignment for New York's touchdown assault when it was exonerated after one play. Gifford, trying to run a sweep into the end zone, fumbled, and Don Joyce smothered the ball with all of his 255-pound body.

No one was happier than assistant coach John Bridges. Before the game began, he gave special instructions to linebacker Don Shinnick and defensive tackle Big Daddy Lipscomb. He did so at the last minute as both were preparing to take the field on the Giants first possession of the game.

"He came up to Big Daddy and me and told us when the Giants pull both their guards, they don't usually block the tackle, and sometimes they come back with a run through the middle," explained Shinnick. "He told Big Daddy that, instead of following the guard, to charge straight into the hole. And he told me to move up and fill Big Daddy's place on the line of scrimmage.

"We hadn't practiced that all week, and it seemed strange that Bridges would wait to say anything about it until just before the game. It worked, though. We caused Gifford to fumble on the 10-yard line, and Joyce recovered for us."

Gifford trudged off the field disillusioned after his second fumble, a somewhat tarnished idol in front of the hometown fans who adored him. He sat alone on the bench with his thoughts and needed the solitude away from the action on the field to reflect on what went wrong.

"I really felt bad about that one," recalled a remorseful Gifford. "We were going in for the score, but the Colts took it away. If I had to pick a spot where the game began to turn, that was it."

Unitas made sure of that. Did he ever. This time he made use of his golden arm. He saddled the Colts on a vintage fifteen-play, 86-yard gallop into the Giants end zone. It began obnoxiously with an errant pass to Dupre. But then Unitas caught fire. He found Berry for the first time with a simple 5-yard throw. On third down, he used a flare to Ameche for 10 yards and a first down on the Colts 29. Moore then got another one to the 39.

When Ameche gained 6 yards and Moore 4, the Colts had another first down. Ameche got across midfield with a 2-yard gain to the Giants 49. Unitas connected with Berry but the lithe receiver was ruled out of bounds. Facing a third and 7, Unitas needed a big play. Dropping to pass, he couldn't find anyone open and took off. He scrambled for 16 yards before being corralled on the Giants 30.

The Colts momentarily bogged down. After Moore couldn't get more than a yard, Baltimore was beset with a 5-yard in-motion penalty. From the 34, Unitas searched for Berry and found him with a 13-yard strike to the 21. On a vital third down, Ameche contributed a first with a 6-yard burst to the 15. Unitas, a matador in cleats, went for the kill. He got it with a touchdown pass to Berry that he knifed between two Giants defenders that gave the Colts a 14–3 advantage and consumed eight minutes of the clock. With just over a minute left until halftime, the Giants ran off three meaningless plays from their 20-yard line.

The Giants had to make adjustments both for an offense that was nonexistent and for a defense that turned soft in spots. Assistant coach Vince Lombardi had one solution. He detected that the Colts defense, which had been brilliant in the first two quarters, had been keying on Gifford. It was flawlessly working except for one play in the opening quarter. Lombardi suggested using Gifford as a decoy. Although the Giants had been outplayed, they still were in reach, even though they had done nothing on offense.

Apprehension was on the faces of the Giants faithful. Unitas was on his game, completing all but four passes, and the one that he misfired on, Berry was ruled out of bounds. Compounding the local fans' fear was that the Colts were to receive the second-half kickoff, and Unitas would be right there again. It wasn't a pleasant thought.

He began the way he left off on the Colts last touchdown. After a 5-yard advance by Moore, Unitas fired an 8-yard dart to Jim Mutscheller and a first down on the Colts 32. However, on the next play, Giants linebacker Harland Svare read a reverse and upended the speedy Moore for a 7-yard loss. Unitas's second-down call turned volatile. He found Berry near the sideline and hit him with a 15-yard throw. Huff ran him hard out of bounds and unleashed his frustrations in a heated exchange with Ewbank that almost resulted in a fight as Shinnick came over to help his coach.

Dupre apparently got a first down, but his 3-yard run was offset by an offside penalty. Unitas came right back to him with a pass, but Dupre was 4 yards short of a first down. The Colts punted, and Don Maynard's 9-yard runback put the ball in play on New York's 21-yard line.

The Giants, with high expectations for the first time on offense, showed nothing. It was almost embarrassing. Gifford got nothing. Conerly then lobbed him a pass in the flat that lost 3 yards. When Conerly looked to pass, he was buried for a 5-yard loss on the 13. The Giants were in trouble. Baltimore would get the ball in striking distance for another score.

Chandler came through with a booming clutch punt that Moore could only fair catch on the Colts 41-yard line. But that was good enough field position for Unitas to operate from. If he could get the Colts another touchdown, the spirit of the Giants players would be broken, as well as the hearts of their fans.

With that in mind, Unitas, going for the jugular, looked off Berry and opened with a 32-yard strike to Mutscheller on the Giants 27-yard line. His fake to Berry caught the Giants off guard. In one seemingly effortless throw, he had positioned the Colts to register their third touchdown and probably the deciding one. There was no way the docile Giants offense could produce three touchdowns. Not from what they showed so far.

The yell of "Dee-Fense" reverberated after Dupre picked up a yard. When Unitas threw incomplete to Berry, the noise got louder. But then Unitas quieted them with an 11-yarder to Berry and a first down on the 15. He came back with a quick pass to Moore for 12 more yards and another first down on the 3-yard line to the groan of thousands. This was Ameche territory, and the punishing fullback made it to the 1. When Unitas was stuffed on a quarterback sneak, he turned once again to Ameche. The Horse tried the middle and found nothing.

On fourth down, Unitas looked over his shoulder at the Colts bench. He briskly brushed off sending in Myhra to attempt what appeared to be a sure field goal and a 17–3 Colts lead. Touchdowns were always first with Unitas. That had always been his mantra, and more often than not Unitas produced them.

His thought was to engage in a bit of chicanery with Ameche. He would take the snap, turn to his right, and flip the ball to Ameche, who would toss an easy pass to Mutscheller in the end zone. Ameche blew the play. Instead, he ran right into the clutches of Livingston, who dropped him for a loss on the 5-yard line.

"Alan never did explain why he didn't throw," Unitas later revealed. "He knew that was the play."

It made no difference to Robustelli. The bottom line was that the defense stopped them.

"You could see it in their eyes, by the way they walked and reacted," said Robustelli about the Colts. "We had taken their best shot, and it had failed. So they became unsure, off-balance, and we had grabbed the momentum in the game."

Huff exhorted the offense to get going as he ran to the sidelines. "There was no way they were going to score," he exclaimed later. "They weren't going to get a damn thing."

But the Giants offense wasn't doing a damn thing either. It was the defense that saved the day for the moment with a heroic goal line stand that had Giants fans screaming and Colts followers stupefied.

Yet what could the Giants' mobilized forces do from the 5-yard line? They couldn't take any risks and conventionally played it safe with a 5-yard run by Gifford and a 3-yard saunter by Webster. Conerly faced a crucial third down as he hunched over the center on the 13-yard line. The Colts braced for the run. The old gunslinger duped them. He crossed up the Colts by dispatching Rote deep, disdaining the short yardage offense the Colts were prepared to stop.

Rote slipped behind the Baltimore secondary, and like Unitas earlier on his pass to Moore, Conerly lofted a pass into his receiver's hands as easily as it was done in practice. Andy Nelson caught Rote from behind to prevent a touchdown and did so with a jarring tackle that caused Rote to fumble. As the horrified throng screamed in despair at the reality of a loose football rolling toward the Colts' goal line, Webster, who was trailing the play, grabbed the ball and was knocked out of bounds by Taseff on the 1-yard line.

Could Baltimore's defense do what the Giants did minutes earlier? For one play they did, when Webster was denied. But on the next play, Triplett went over right guard behind Jack Stroud for the coveted touchdown. In one well-scripted play the Giants came alive. That one wild play had practically matched the Giants entire first-half output. More significantly, the game's momentum changed.

"They were waiting to see what we would do," claimed Huff. They were the ones who were worried. We had it going."

The crowd felt it, too, with deafening roars that followed when the Colts got the ball, leading only 14–10 now. The Giants defense responded by shutting down the Colts on three plays. Dupre could only manufacture 2 yards. But on second down, Modzelewski brought the crowd to its feet by sacking Unitas with a 7-yard loss. Stymied by finding no one open, Unitas had to run for it on third down and managed to collect 9 yards, which was far short of a first down, and Baltimore had to punt.

That stifling series defined the fact that the propulsion had indeed switched to the Giants. Conerly kept it going, starting from the Giants 19-yard line as the third quarter was coming to a close. There was time for just two plays. After Webster rushed for 3 yards, Conerly fooled the Colts defense again. Instead of running out the clock, he dropped back and sent Bob Schnelker over the middle with a 17-yard pass. When the quarter ended, Conerly had taken the Giants to the 39.

The Marlboro Man was in a groove. With his first two plays in the fourth quarter, he displayed how much. He faked to Gifford and connected with Schnelker with a 46-yard bomb to Baltimore's 15-yard line. Near pandemonium filled the stadium. Giants fans had their own Unitas. With the Colts defense in disarray, Conerly moved quickly. He called his buddy Gifford's number and executed a perfect pass for the touchdown that sent the Giants ahead and the crowd near delirium. The noise resonated into the darkness of the Bronx sky. Babe Ruth never created a bigger one. *Sports Illustrated*'s pro football maven,

Tex Maule, described the noise as "something you could not believe—a wall of sound." After all, it was New York.

But, still, they didn't have Unitas. Starting from his own 20-yard line, he got the Colts moving. He connected with Moore for 11 yards and with Berry for 13. He tried for Dupre but missed. He picked up a yard when he was chased out of the pocket by Frank Youso, who was filling in admirably for the injured Grier.

On third down, Unitas went to the dependable Mutscheller. His pass was ruled complete on the Giants 38 when interference was flagged on Crow. Following a 1-yard loss by Ameche, Unitas went back to the air. He went deep to Dupre but couldn't connect. When he tried to deliver a quick one to Moore in the middle, Huff denied him. Rechichar replaced Myhra to attempt a game-tying 46-yard field goal. His kick fell to the ground harmlessly short.

◆

The Colts remained 3 points behind with some ten minutes left in what would come down to a battle of wills: a spunky Colts team against the proud Giants with their championship banners wafting in the breeze from the bleacher flag pole. All they needed for another one was to play defense like they had done so wonderfully and run out the clock on offense. It was a highly workable scenario, with Conerly on one side of the ball and Huff on the other.

But they had to keep the ball from Unitas. He was special. The Giants knew it, too. And so, they went to work on offense, determined to keep the ball out of Unitas's hands. The way the defense was playing, they didn't need any more points. They needed only to keep Unitas on the sidelines, where he couldn't hurt them anymore.

Things were going the Giants' way. From their 20-yard line, they began working on the clock. Phil King, in relief of a tired Webster, ran for 4 yards. Conerly picked up a first down on the next play with a 15-yard completion to Ken MacAfee. From that point on, Conerly kept it on the ground. Gifford lost 2 yards, but Triplett made up for some of it with a 7-yard gain. It was Gifford again, and this time he found open turf around right end for a 10-yard jaunt to the Colts 46. When he produced 4 more yards on the same play, the Giants were approaching field goal area. However, King obliterated it with a fumble that Krouse recovered back on the Giants 42-yard line.

Unitas took one look at the clock and then looked downfield. He was after a touchdown on the first play and dispatched Moore on a fly pattern. Moore eluded Crow and Tunnell, came down with Unitas's pass on the goal line, and rolled out of bounds as the crowd in that section of the end zone leaped to its feet. Was it a touchdown? Moore looked up and saw the referee signal no. He ruled that Moore was out of bounds when he caught the ball. Moore demonstratively insisted that he wasn't, but to no avail.

"I was in bounds, I was, dammit, I really was," Moore claimed for years whenever he was asked about the play.

When Karilivacz knocked down a pass intended for Berry, the Giants appeared out of danger. But there was Unitas again. He collaborated with Berry for 11 yards and a first down on the Giants 31. Dupre got the Colts closer for a tying field goal with a 4-yard run to the 27. The Giants defense erupted with fury. First, the forcible Robustelli dropped Unitas for an 11-yard loss. Then, the irresistible Modzelewski followed with a 9-yard loss, and suddenly, from two herculean plays, the Colts had retreated to the 47, the field goal gone and their chances of winning severely diminished with only 2:30 left.

"At that point, we just had to keep the ball, run out the clock, and they'd never get another chance," explained Alex Webster afterwards. "We were so hot. Everything was working well. It sure looked like our game."

It appeared that way to Donovan, too. "You bet your ass we were worried," he confessed. "We're thinking, 'Here we go all over again.' A lot of us had never won four games in a season in our career. Now, we're almost going to win the championship, and we were blowing it. I was saying a Hail Mary."

With the clock winding down, the Giants started to work on it with Webster's 5-yard run from the 19. The Colts finally caught Gifford on a sweep and stopped him for no gain. Conerly was challenged by a key third-down call to keep the ball. He alertly observed Baltimore playing the run and finessed them with a 10-yard ace to Webster and a big first down.

At that moment in the press box, the writers had voted Conerly as the game's most valuable player. The Giants were only one first down away from a title. Webster got a yard, and Gifford on a sweep added 5 more. On third and 4, Conerly crouched over his center with the biggest play of the game for the Giants. He wanted his sidekick Gifford to deliver the first down and the victory from the Giants 35.

It was a vintage running play that was a vital part of the Giants' arsenal and was prosperous all year long. Gifford would take the handoff from Conerly and start to go wide behind his pulling guards. If Marchetti crashed, then Gifford would cut back inside. Marchetti read the play and forced Gifford to alter his run. Lipscomb halted his pursuit and quickly reversed himself to close what was a big enough hole for Gifford's advance. Marchetti grabbed a piece of Gifford, but Lipscomb, all 288 pounds of him, followed by Shinnick, smothered the Giants runner. Marchetti was on the bottom of the pile of bodies when

Lipscomb landed on his leg and snapped it like a dry twig right above the ankle.

Marchetti's cry of pain created a whistle for a time-out without anyone knowing if Gifford had reached the 40-yard line for a precious first down. It appeared that he had, but none of the officials gave the signal that would have created a volcano of cheers from Giants fans. The crowd with clutched hands waited.

"Frank was hollering," disclosed Marchetti. "I guess he thought I was lying there faking it to get an additional time-out. 'Get your damn butt off the ground, Gino.' I was down. The play is over. I said, 'Frank, I can't get up. I can't.'"

There was momentary chaos on the field as a stretcher carried off Marchetti. He ordered the stretcher bearers to put him down by the goal line because he wanted to watch the end of the game. "As captain, I thought it was important to be there," remarked Gino. When referee Charley Berry placed the ball, Gifford was inches short of the game-clinching first down.

"All this hollering is going on, and Gifford's saying, 'I made the first down. I made the sticks,'" was the way Donovan described it. "Hell, he didn't even get back to the line of scrimmage."

But Gifford insisted he did, even to this day. That one play decided the outcome of what has been written by pro football historians as the greatest game ever played. And, from the standpoints of dramatics alone, it was.

"I made the first down," swore Gifford. "I know I made it. But Marchetti broke his leg and was screaming like a wounded panther. There was a lot of confusion. A lot of time passed while they carried Marchetti off the field. When they spotted the ball, it was placed short of the first-down marker. I saw the referee pick it up at his front foot, but he put it down where his back foot was."

Rote concurred. He was near the play and walked over to Berry, who was holding the ball.

"The referee was so concerned about Marchetti that he forgot where he picked up the ball," explained Rote. "I saw him pick it up with his front foot, but he put it down where his back foot was."

It was a matter of inches short of a first down, and Giants players wanted to go for it. Several pleaded with Howell, but Howell decided not to. His thinking was sound. He had the league's leading punter in Don Chandler, who was proficient in booting, high, booming kicks, and because of the hang time they produced, most of his punts weren't run back. Players in battle get emotional at some point in a game, and in a highly charged one like this, a coach has to temper feeling with logic. A fourth-down play was a gamble. A punt was not.

The Giants' players slammed their helmets to the ground in disgust. When Chandler exploded a 43-yard punt that Taseff had to fair catch on the 14, Howell's decision appeared correct. There was only 1:56 left when Unitas undertook the biggest challenge of his three-year career. Less than two minutes to conquer 86 yards of earth. It would prove to be the defining moment of Unitas's entire existence. There was excitement in his eyes, which were sharp and alert despite the tense struggle, because he knew his mission.

"The goal posts were so far back they looked like they were in Baltimore," recalled Unitas.

A chilly mist began to envelope the field as the teams lined up. Everyone knew that Unitas would throw and throw, and he was so good at it. The Giants aligned their defensive mechanism to abort the big play that would yield chunks of terrain. When Unitas missed on his first two passes, one to Mutscheller and another to Dupre, the Giants players raised their helmets high on the crowded sidelines, which now numbered more people than players, coaches, and equipment personnel. But Unitas uncurled a bullet to Moore in the center of the Giants phalanx for an 11-yard first down. He would have a fresh set of downs. That's all he needed.

Ray Berry, a slow-footed receiver by pro standards, had weak vision that required contacts, a corset to protect a bad back, and one leg shorter than the other, which he compensated for by having one shoe with long cleats. But Unitas had confidence in him, and that's all that mattered.

There was one thing that Berry excelled at, and that was he ran precise patterns and had sure hands, two traits that Unitas admired and why over the years he became Unitas's favorite receiver. The other quality that was not lost on the quarterback was that Berry wasn't afraid of patterns that took him into the middle of the field, knowing that he would be battered by a linebacker or a defensive back, sometimes at the same moment of impact. In Tunnell and Patton, the Giants had two safeties who could punish a receiver.

Unitas and Berry were two warriors welded into one spirit. In the twelve years they eventually would be together, Berry looked back at this afternoon as the most significant of all the hundreds of passes he caught from Unitas. "It certainly was the best game that Unitas and I had together," he said.

Unitas analyzed that the Giants were defending the deep ball by protecting the sidelines. That left the middle vulnerable. That meant Berry. Unitas realized the middle was his to exploit when Moore was wide open on the third-down pass that gave the Colts a first down on the 25. Still, Unitas needed to negotiate at least 45 more yards for a game-tying field goal attempt from a kicker who wasn't all that good. Berry was his guy alright. He caught a 25-yard pass at midfield with 1:04 left, then another at the sidelines for 15 more. He repeated the play and got an additional 22 yards to the Giants 13.

Like a burglar, Unitas stole everything the Giants laid before him, and he took it without the least bit of hesitation with his accomplice, the irrepressible Berry. It was a virtuoso lesson in cleats on a soggy field, Unitas to Berry again and again, never missing a note. It was Leonard Bernstein at the Met, Joe DiMaggio's grace in embracing a fly ball on the very same field that left a hypnotized crowd in awe and Sam Huff and the Giants defense in frustration. Public address announcer Bob Sheppard's voice reverberated throughout the stadium, "Unitas to Berry." It was Napoleon at Waterloo, Custer at Big Horn, Lee at Gettysburg, and Huff carried that in his sleep for all those fifty years of December nightmares.

Huff will never forget the sequence, three consecutive completions to Berry that produced 62 yards, two-thirds of a football field. Baltimore was threatening at the closed end of Yankee Stadium, where Babe Ruth once stood at home plate and with a mighty swing delivered majestic home runs to a delirious crowd.

Gifford was standing next to Conerly intently looking on, hoping for a Giants defense to respond just one more time. "I hope this doesn't go into overtime because I can't go anymore," confided a tired Conerly.

Was it possible what Unitas had done? In just over a minute he had taken the Colts 73 yards to position the 3 points necessary to tie the game. A championship game. And he did it with audibles because there wasn't any precious time to waste in huddles. Only seven seconds remained when the shaky Myhra looked up at the goal posts to deliver the biggest kick of his life, close to where Ruth had stood.

His kick would end the game one way or the other. If he was accurate, there would be overtime. If he missed, which he did quite often, Conerly and his buddies would celebrate at Toots Shor's until dawn. The Colts still needed respectability. They needed the field goal. Myhra gave them both and at the same time chased the monkey off his back with a 19-yard field goal, 17–17.

"I told myself I better not miss it, or it was going to be a long, cold winter on the farm in North Dakota," he said.

For Unitas and the Colts, it was utopia, a kind of valentine that everyone embraced, even Giants fans, who certainly were impressed by the virtuoso performance. What Baltimore had just done would change pro football—the dynamic two-minute offense.

The game had been heroically contested, but there would be even more drama and more heroics in overtime. By now, it was dark, and the weather, which was mild when the game started, had turned cold. Patches of ice appeared in some places on the field, and the players huddled under their capes on the sidelines.

A five-minute respite was all the players would get. There wasn't enough time to take refuge in the dressing rooms as they waited for the coin toss to determine who would get the ball first. The Giants called it correctly and breathed a lot easier. After what Unitas had just done, they didn't want to face him again. But he still loomed menacingly on the sidelines. The Giants had to score to keep him there.

By now both teams showed signs of weariness from the tense, grudging battle. If anything, the Colts had the benefit of an extra week's rest. What's more, they had Unitas.

The Giants began the overtime shakily. Maynard fumbled Rechichar's kick on the 10-yard line but managed to recover on the 20. With only ten first downs the entire game, Conerly needed to create some big plays for the Giants to win, but he was tired. There he was, a cowboy needing one last ride. He tried to do it himself after Gifford opened with a 4-yard run. However, he missed with a pass to Schnelker and came up a yard short trying to fool the Colts on a keeper play. Chandler had to punt, and that meant the defense would have to face Unitas again. It was a sobering thought.

Chandler did his best to help with a huge punt, so high that Taseff could only return it 1 yard to the 20. Unitas had to cover 80 yards, or at least 60, to produce the winning points. Like Toscanini at Carnegie Hall, he wouldn't miss a note. Unitas would be a maestro in high-top shoes. His baton was his priceless right arm, and he would direct a superlative thirteen-play drive that established the beginning of his legendary status. In the process, he would convert two critical third-down challenges to accomplish his objective of bringing a championship to Baltimore.

Unitas's first pass was an 8-yard completion to Ameche. On the second, he relied on Berry and advanced the Colts a yard short of midfield with a 21-yard sideline toss. Next, he demonstrated his uncanny field perception. Seeing that the Giants second line of defense had split to help on pass coverage, he pointed to Ameche in the huddle to run a trap play. Ameche responded, gaining 22 yards and reaching New York's 20-yard line.

"Huff was playing for a pass, and the way Modzelewski was crashing, I figured they were right for a trap," was the way Unitas explained the call. "I hit it right. Hell, they had been blowing in on me pretty hard on pass plays. They were coming up the middle, so I called a trip, and Alan did the rest of it. It wasn't any great call."

Still, Unitas was not thinking field goal, not after Dupre failed to gain a yard. His mindset was touchdown, and he indicated as much with a 12-yard pass in the flat to Berry. Unitas could see the goal posts now. They were only 8 yards away, and Ewbank sent in word to Unitas, who had brought them this far, to play it safe and keep the ball on the ground.

Unitas did keep it on the ground—for one play—when the weary but audacious Giants defense held Ameche to a yard. Unitas wanted more, and he got it with a daring 6-yard pass to Mutscheller, who was driven out of bounds on the 1-yard line. The pugnacious call made the Giants wary of a pass on third down. This was Unitas, the maestro, who had enough confidence to throw one even from the 1-yard line.

Down deep, Unitas didn't trust Myhra and would have no part of a field goal attempt. Myhra had had a bad year, and Unitas didn't want to use him, didn't want to give him a chance. Nobody wanted to trust him with the win. Unitas made sure of it.

He embarrassingly fooled the Giants with his next play. Instead of having Ameche run behind Parker, he sent him to the other side toward guard Alex Sandusky and tackle George Preas. It was a brilliant call. Sandusky and Preas executed to perfection and opened a monstrous hole for Ameche. Perhaps out of amazement, The Horse crossed the goal line and fell into the end zone from his own momentum. The Colts were champions, 23–17. Poetically, it was thirteen plays to glory.

Ameche ran into the open arms of a half-dozen Colts fans, who lifted him into the air like a big teddy bear. There wasn't a need for the extra point; Colts fans took care of that. They tore down the goal posts in a matter of minutes. Their enthusiasm demonstrated how completely pro football had arrived.

All the motion and celebration below left the press box up above in eerie silence. The newspaper strike accounted for that. There wasn't the noise of countless typewriters except for one from an out-of-town sportswriter.

"Listen," he told respected columnist Art Daley of the *New York Times,* "if the noise of this typewriter disturbs you, just let me know. I don't want to embarrass you."

The ever circumspective Unitas didn't get trapped by all the boisterous well-wishers on the field. As soon as Ameche crossed the goal line, he ran into the third-base dugout and the safety of the dressing room.

The *Sport* magazine red Corvette that was heading into Conerly's garage was Unitas's now. A club official informed the quarterback that Ed Sullivan wanted him on his show. His performance was that good. But Unitas flatly turned down the offer. He wanted to be with his team on their return flight to Baltimore. Ameche went instead and picked up $500 for his appearance.

—

The victory changed the fatalistic feeling of Colts fans and the city's stigma as losers, and the deliverer was Unitas, who was swamped by the media. They wanted to know how he did it, how he took the Colts on two prolific long drives in the waning minutes of regulation and the overtime to script such a dramatic finish. In the crush of the small room, a reporter asked Unitas about what he described as a gambling pass to Mutscheller, risking an interception. Unitas gave him a stern look and answered with calculated assuredness.

"It wasn't a gamble," he snapped. "They didn't see what I saw. When you know what you're doing, you're not intercepted. The Giants were jammed up at the line and not expecting a pass. If Jim had been covered, I'd have thrown the pass out of bounds. It's just that I would rather win a game like this by a touchdown than a field goal. It was no sweat. They were playing one on one, looking for a run. All I had to do was flip it up there for Jim and let him catch it. I don't expect a pass like that to fail, and it didn't. No matter how good a defense is, you can always find a weakness somewhere. You find it and start hitting it. When they close it up, you have to then find the next weakness."

Mutscheller agreed. "There was not really that much danger," he explained. "It was a diagonal-type pass, a 60 diagonal right. I slant out at 45 degrees, and John has to throw it right away. If Crow doesn't follow Moore, it's a touchdown to him."

Unitas just sat calmly answering the questions that kept coming. It seemed that he repeated his answers time after time, but he didn't seem to mind. Not after a game like this. Not after the team's first world championship. This was a golden moment to be cherished. He wasn't in any hurry, and the bus or the plane would never leave without him. Not after what he had done. Unitas continued to explain what made those two dramatic drives work to perfection. And he told them straight out.

"They were just giving us certain things, and we were taking them," he said. "Berry was working back there on Karilivacz deep on his outside, and then we'd come back inside and work on a linebacker. They were just leaving it there, so we kept going back to it, taking advantage of it. We could just as easily have gone to the other side, but when you got something like that going, you just don't give it up. We were also beating the linebacker, Svare. We'd beat him deep, go behind him, and we'd throw it in front of him next. Huff was concerned about that little quick slant-in on the weak side, and he was trying to help Svare and Karilivacz. But he should have never gotten out of the middle. If you can take care of your own responsibilities first and then go back and help there, too, fine, but he couldn't do both things at the same time. He never should have gotten so far out of his position. When he did that, he just left open the big trap play in the middle for Ameche."

Marchetti never got to see the winning touchdown. He sat alone in the Colts dressing room without either a TV or a radio, but he would have preferred remaining on the field.

"I wouldn't let them take me into the clubhouse at first," claimed Marchetti. "This was my game, too. I watched as we drove to Myhra's field goal. But they were afraid we'd be over-run by the crowd. When I didn't hear much noise, I knew we were moving. Then the door flew open, and one of our safeties came running in. Before he yelled, I knew we had won it. The crowd was very quiet."

Minutes later, Ewbank walked over to Marchetti and pre-sented him with the game ball. He was one of the heroes, but he was humble with the honor.

"Hell, I oughta cut this thing up in fifty pieces," he remarked without hesitation. "I never saw a game that had so much. So many players who made such big plays."

Unitas had willed the victory and made those around him respond with confidence.

"Johnny told us in the huddle before we began that drive that we were going to take the ball right down and score," con-fided Ameche. "And we all believed him."

Berry, too, was a believer.

"We all got our confidence from Johnny," he praised. "I can't explain it, but I absolutely knew that we were going to score on that drive. As we ran onto the field, John had this kind of detached look like, 'Okay, let's get this thing over with.'"

Donovan was in a happy mood. He was always one for a good story, and he had those around him laughing with his latest.

"I had more problems before the game than during it," he began. "My father and my best friend, John Brady, were sitting on the Colts bench. Brady was a police captain and responsible for security for the game. He had a bottle and got drunk. He kept passing the bottle to my father. I said, "Cut it out, Jack. I got enough problems on the field without having to worry about my father getting drunk."

There was little consolation in the Giants quarters, where Gifford was searching for answers. He cried openly. Lombardi bent over and offered some comforting words. "We wouldn't have gotten here without you," he said. It didn't help. Gifford was haunted by the two fumbles that he felt cost the Giants the victory and the championship. And he was still agonizing over his third-down run that was inches short of a first down.

Jack Stroud was still visibly upset as he stood in front of his locker.

"We only needed 4 inches," he said. "We would have run through a brick wall at that point. Besides, Marchetti was out, and whoever they put in for him couldn't have been as good. He would have been nervous, tight, and ready for it to happen to him. It would have gone to him, and dammit, it would have worked."

Jack Mara, the president of the Giants, couldn't believe Berry's performance, especially from someone who had such poor eyesight and wore thick glasses off the field and contact lenses to play.

"Berry is so blind that the only thing he can see is a football," remarked Mara whimsically.

Ken Kavanaugh, the Giants assistant coach, saw Gifford's first down from his vantage point high above the playing field.

"I saw Gifford's first down attempt real good," Kavanaugh said. "When he hit the ground, he looked as if he was 2 feet over the first-down marker. The head linesman came up and brought it back 2 feet. I was yelling downstairs to Jim Lee Howell. I said he put the ball back too far. I could see it. All we were looking for was a first down, and we could have run the clock out."

While the Giants missed by inches, Unitas made them count. A number of quarterbacks could throw deep, but the difference was that Unitas could pass long. Those inches in his fluid arm are the difference between a thrower and a passer. But the complete quarterback is the one who can think. Unitas won every inch of that game with his head.

"The man was a genius," marveled Huff. "I never saw a quarterback that good on those two drives. You couldn't stop the Unitas-to-Berry combination. It just seemed like Unitas to Berry, Unitas to Berry, over and over again, like a nightmare. We were a great team, but we played against a better team."

The years haven't healed Huff's pain. They never will because in the span of two minutes, the Giants had lost a championship. And in those two minutes, Unitas created a new weapon, the two-minute offense.

He did so with refreshing humility, as if to say he was expected to do so. He had to prove himself all his football life.

"I just got a chance to show my stuff," remarked Unitas. "That's all I've needed, but nobody ever gave it to me before."

Evelyn Helm has never forgotten the game she witnessed fifty years ago. Now ninety-four years old and living in Sun City, Arizona, she and her husband, Clifton Callaway, a naval officer at the time, had season tickets to the Giants the eleven years they lived on Long Island. They were sitting with another couple on the 50-yard line in the lower stands and had talked about the game periodically before Clifton's death in 1985.

"Oh, what an exciting game, one I'll never forget," says Evelyn. "One of the Colt players got hurt, and they removed him on a stretcher. He wouldn't let them remove him from the field. The poor fellow was in so much pain that he was vomiting. I admired what that Baltimore quarterback, Unitas, did, but we were all heartbroken that the Giants lost."

Len Jaffe and his wife, Lois, lifelong New Yorkers, were sitting in the upper deck that day, newlyweds since October. By the fourth quarter, the temperature had dropped almost 20 degrees, and Lenny began to feel it in both his feet. To this day, Jaffe swears Gifford made the crucial first down and was so upset that he didn't immediately answer his wife when she asked about it.

"I was locked in with my binoculars and had a perfect view of the referee marking the ball," claimed Jaffe. "I saw where Gifford was brought down. He made the first down. I couldn't believe where the referee spotted the ball. It cost us the game."

Yet, above all others, it was a moment that Colts fan eighty-three-year-old Romeo Valianti will always cherish. When he lived in Westminster, he was a regular at the Colts preseason camp and became close with a number of the players, especially Ameche, Unitas, and even Ewbank. The coach gave him a field pass to the game, which Valianti clung to on the train ride from Baltimore.

"Stick with me," ordered Ewbank before the kickoff.

Valianti did just that and more. He went over to Marchetti when he was taken off the field on a stretcher in the fourth quarter. When the game ended, he secured a piece of the wooden goal post that was torn down and dug up some dirt where Ameche scored the winning touchdown. He took it back with him to Baltimore and made a planter and gave it to Ameche.

"I asked Ameche in the dressing room if he could appear at a Knights of Columbus dinner that we were giving for kids the next night," recalled Valianti. "Ameche said he didn't know, there was so much going on. The next evening, he showed up at my house."

Minutes later, Valianti took a phone message from *Sports Illustrated* for Unitas.

"Take it and make believe it's me," joked Unitas.

"I can't do that," remarked Valianti.

"You didn't think we would lose, did you, Romeo?" asked Unitas.

"Yes, I did," admitted Valianti.

"Well, I didn't," Unitas assured him.

❧

The huge newspaper strike ended at midnight, and at midafternoon, Joe Trimble of the *New York Daily News* was given the opportunity to view film of the game with Jim Lee Howell. He left satisfied and wrote the following in Tuesday's edition:

Well, it seems the Giants did not make that crucial first down a couple of minutes from the end of the fourth period at the stadium Sunday. Frank Gifford thought he had it and so did the Giants coaches, but film showed it was a near-miss, unfortunate and expensive.

Anyway, judging from the films, head linesman Charley Berry didn't make a mistake. The third-down play shows Gifford reaching the New York 43-yard line, plus maybe a few inches. He didn't appear to reach the 44, which was necessary for the first down. Howell stopped the action and re-ran it a couple of times, almost in hope Giff might get that needed distance. But each time the play ended, Frank was in the same place.

The coach shook his head. We thought he made it all right, but it doesn't show there. And, it happened right in front of our bench.

❧

Tex Maule sat before his typewriter to write the cover story for *Sports Illustrated*. But before he began, he went into the office of Sid James, the magazine's managing editor.

"What do you think about it?" asked James.

"It may have been the greatest football game ever played," answered Maule without hesitation.

"Hey, that's the lead," exclaimed James. "Go with it."

Actually, it appeared in print as the best, not the greatest. James thought it over and felt that *greatest* was overused in sports jargon.

$$\bullet$$

No matter what word was appropriate, the game justified it.

Fifty years later, it has never been equaled.

EPILOGUE

We didn't know it at the time, but it was the beginning for us. From that game forward, our fan base grew. We owe both franchises a great debt.

—NFL Commissioner Pete Rozelle

Johnny Unitas wasn't aware of the impact that the overtime win over the Giants had created. If he did, he wasn't saying anything or little at all. Being the competitor he was, his only concern was about winning a football game. That's how he accepted it. It was that way ever since he was a kid at St. Justin's and later at Louisville, even to the sandlots of the Bloomfield Rams.

He was even that way when playing cards with his teammates, which he wasn't very good at, and they would take his money with appreciation. Unitas was the fiber champions are made of and shrugged off any reference to the records he established that long afternoon. The Colts won, 23–17, and they were champions and got their respect. That's all that mattered to him.

"The biggest thing I remember about that game," Unitas said a month later, "was some drunk suddenly appearing on the field and the New York cops chasing him all over Yankee Stadium. They finally collared the guy, but when they were taking him away, he yelled, 'Damn, don't bother with me. Grab that guy wearing number 19. He's the guy that's killing us.'"

That's how unaffected he was about playing and winning the biggest game of his life. He was, in the true meaning of the term, a consummate pro. And brutally honest, too. There was only 1:56 left in the game, and the cold, gray mist had further dampened Unitas's chance for a miracle that was 86 yards away. Insurmountable odds. But not to Unitas.

"We had the game locked up in the third," reflected Unitas, "and it looked like we had blown it. We were so damn disgusted with ourselves that we struck back at the Giants in a sort of blind fury the last time we got the ball."

But America knew how significant the game was. Unitas had become a national treasure. Every high school quarterback and the ones in college wanted to be like Johnny Unitas. Barbers around the country put down their combs and scissors and began using electric razors to sculpture Unitas crew cuts. High-top shoes were a must for every kid who dreamed about being like Unitas. If there was a cult hero in professional football, it now was Unitas. If he had played for the Giants, his photograph would have adorned a poster in Times Square. But Unitas was just happy playing and winning for Baltimore.

An unknown Lamar Hunt of Dallas realized the significance of the dramatic game. Overnight that one game made pro football big, so big, that Hunt, a bespectacled twenty-six-year-old son of a Texas millionaire whose football background consisted of nothing more than being a third string end with a total of twenty minutes' playing time at SMU, announced the formation of another professional football league. He convinced seven others to join him in forming the American Football League, which was to begin play in 1960. It was a bold move, as big as the size of Texas, when considering that it took decades for the NFL to become established and become solidified on December 28 in Yankee Stadium.

To some degree, Raymond Berry recognized the game's importance. Long after the contest's conclusion, Berry walked out of the stadium and noticed Commissioner Bert Bell, who had marshaled his tenuous legions for fourteen years. Bell had watched the sudden death drama like a fan, sitting at midfield behind the press box with his son, Bert, and daughter, Janie. Before he became commissioner in 1946, he had been a coach and an owner. Bell was happy for Colts owner Carroll Rosenbloom and felt justified knowing he had persuaded Rosenbloom to buy the franchise for Baltimore. It paid off for Rosenbloom and the league.

Bell was doubly satisfied that a five-year-old team such as Baltimore rose so quickly to win a championship ahead of the more established cities. Only months before, in October, Bell appeared in Congress to defend the league's college player draft, which was deemed illegal by opponents. He convinced the lawmakers that the draft was a democratic process that enabled lesser teams to compete with the stronger ones. He enlightened Congress by specially citing Baltimore as an example of becoming a championship contender in such a short period of time. Bell made his points well.

Personally, he was also happy that he had fought with many of the owners when he advocated establishing a sudden death period strictly for a championship game in the event of a tie, such as the one he had just witnessed. And what he and 65,000 in Yankee Stadium, and perhaps ten million more on television, had observed was the best damn football game ever played. Pro football and television formed a union that December day. It was high theater, a monumental struggle, and its catalyst was Unitas, a new hero who was adulated by all who observed him.

When Berry saw Bell standing alone on the sidewalk, he quietly approached him. Berry was a big reason why the Colts were champions, as his twelve receptions and 178 yards were both new title game records. That didn't occupy his mind at that moment. Bell did. His thoughts were with the short, solitary figure that he wanted to address. In his own quiet way, Berry wanted to pay him a tribute.

"Here was a guy who had midwifed the NFL and shepherded it through all the tough times," recognized Berry. "I walked up to shake his hand, and he had tears in his eyes. He knew what the game meant. The rest of us, we had no perception of the big picture. But the commissioner, he knew his baby grew up that day."

Hours before, Bell had mentioned to a writer that he thought he would never live to see sudden death, but he did. Sadly, he died a year later, and, fittingly, while attending the Eagles–Steelers game in Franklin Field in his hometown of Philadelphia on October 11. It was surreal. He suffered a heart attack during the final two minutes of the game, the same amount of time Unitas used only the year before to force the first overtime, Bell's overtime, in Yankee Stadium.

The Unitas-to-Berry artistry left an indelible memory. Unitas, too, had established new records with his magnificent performance in completing twenty-six of forty passes for 349 yards, both new championship game marks. Yet Unitas appeared unaffected by it and by all the stories that were written or all the radio talk heralding the overtime thriller as the greatest game ever played. For the still-growing NFL and its fans, it was. But not exactly to Unitas. A frank and honest individual, he demonstrated those qualities by admitting that he got a bigger bang beating the San Francisco 49ers that season in Baltimore, 35–27, on a bitter cold afternoon.

"I got a bigger thrill in helping to win that game that got us into the playoffs," confessed Unitas while relaxing in a Baltimore hotel room. "We trailed at halftime, 27–7, but we got hot in the second half, offensively and defensively, and won. If we hadn't, we would never have had the chance at the championship.

"It was only 24 degrees, and my hands were numb. The cold had never bothered me like it did that day. There were times when I couldn't even feel the ball. I usually try to rough up my fingertips on the wall in the locker room or on the dirt to make them more sensitive on such days, even on days when it's not so cold, but nothing seemed to have any effect during the first half. The ball just dropped right out of my hands on one occasion. Although it kept getting colder, I finally was able to warm up in the second half. Lenny Moore's 73-yard touchdown run did it for us in the fourth quarter. He really scooted.

"The place was bedlam when Steve Myhra booted home the extra point to put us ahead, 28–27. After that, it was anticlimatic. We drove for another touchdown. I threw an 8-yarder to Berry that tied me with Cecil Isbell's record of having one touchdown pass in twenty-three straight games. To tell you the truth, I didn't even care. I knew we had won the title.

"I think most of the drama in the Giants game came from the championship setting rather than the game itself. We came down to tie it in the final seconds. Then it became the first playoff game ever to go into sudden death. You can't have much more drama than that."

Art Donovan felt the same way as Unitas about the San Francisco game, and he's always been one to speak his mind.

"That was the greatest game I've ever played in," he admitted. "We were getting killed, but we came back and annihilated them to win our first division championship. That was something.

"You can call the Giants game the most important game ever played because it may have been the best thing to ever happen to the NFL. The whole country was watching it on TV. It wasn't just local. That's the game that put the league over the hump."

Kyle Rote, the Giants versatile receiver, saw it that way, too.

"Everything came together then for the greatness of pro football," felt Rote. "New York is the heartbeat of the media, including Madison Avenue, where the commercial dollar is. Those ad men were young guys—young and sharp—and suddenly they happened to tie into pro football just when television advertising was hitting its peak."

That one game set up professional football as a television sport, and in the following years, the networks began to create technical innovations that added to the visual appeal that sport already presented. Technology such as slow motion, instant replay, and isolated zoom-in camera close-ups made the sport an art form and widened the appeal for the game. The union of pro football and television became so perfect that it honestly presented a clearer and more accurate perspective to the viewer than to someone sitting in the stands.

"Technology land," was how Norman Mailer described it.

Pro football has evolved over the last fifty years as arguably the nation's number one sport and earned its panache after decades of struggle. In the first thirty years, the NFL proceeded with difficulty in the shadow of college football, baseball, and boxing. But in 1958, the sport had matured in the very heart of baseball that was Yankee Stadium.

"That game," described Pulitzer Prize-winning author David Halberstam, "was a watershed event for professional football, for sports in general, for this country. It is not hyperbole to say our lives changed forever that afternoon."

The 1958 championship game played that day between the Colts and the Giants was the beginning of the modern NFL. What they did there that day was incarnated in Pro Football's Hall of Fame, where seventeen players from that game are enshrined.

APPENDIX: FINAL FIGURES

Play-By-Play

FIRST QUARTER

Giants win toss and elect to receive.
Rechichar kicks off to Maynard who downs it in the end-zone.

Giants
1-10-G20 – Heinrich's pass for Rote blocked by Marchetti.
2-10-G20 – Heinrich passes to Webster for 7.
3-03-G27 – Heinrich's pass incomplete for Rote (Taseff).
4-03-G27 – Chandler punts to Taseff on 30, fair catch.

Colts
1-10-C30 – Moore loses 3 on sweep (Karilivacz).
2-13-C27 – Ameche plunges for 7.
3-06-C34 – Unitas fumbles after hit by Huff on pass attempt and Patton recovers on Colts 37.

Giants
1-10-C37 – Webster stopped for loss of 1.
2-11-C38 – Heinrich fumbles after hit by Marchetti, who recovers for Colts on 45.

Colts
1-10-C45 – Unitas hits Dupre for 4.
2-06-C49 – Dupre slams over tackle for 1.

3-05-C50 – Unitas's pass for Berry is intercepted by Crow, who returns 5 to Giants 45.

Giants

1-10-G45 – Gifford loses 1 over right tackle.
2-11-G44 – Triplett stopped for no gain.
3-11-G44 – Heinrich passes to Triplett over the middle for 6.
4-05-G50 – Chandler punts to Taseff on the 8, returns 7.

Colts

1-10-C15 – Unitas hits Moore deep for 60 yards as Patton pulls him down from behind on Giants 25.
1-10-G25 – Ameche powers over right guard for 5.
2-05-G20 – Dupre is stopped for loss of 1 at left end.
3-06-G21 – Delay of game against Colts. 5 yard penalty.
3-11-G26 – Moore gains 2 around right end.
4-09-G24 – Myhra's FG attempt is wide but Giants offside.
4-04-G19 – Myhra's FG attempt from 27 blocked by Huff and recovered by Katcavage on 22.

Giants

1-10-G22 – Conerly at quarterback. Webster for no gain.
2-10-G22 – Conerly passes on a flare to Triplett for 9.
3-01-G31 – Gifford breaks free around left end for 38.
1-10-C31 – Triplett over left side for 2.
2-08-C29 – Conerly's pass for Rote is incomplete.
3-08-C29 – Conerly's pass for Webster is no good as Webster slips and falls.
4-08-C29 – Summerall kicks FG from 36.

Time: 2:02.
Giants 3   Colts 0

Chandler kicks off to Lyles on the 2, returns 19.

Colts
1-10-C21 – Unitas passes to Moore for 5.
2-05-C26 – Dupre over left side for 3.
3-02-C29 – Unitas fails to hit Moore as Crow defends.
4-02-C29 – Brown punts to Crow on Giants 28 and he loses 10 on return as period ends.

SECOND QUARTER

Giants
1-10-G20 – Conerly completes pass to Gifford at left sideline but receiver fumbles. Krouse recovers for Colts on 20.

Colts
1-10-G20 – Moore sweeps right end for 4.
2-06-G16 – Ameche powers over left side for 5.
3-01-G11 – Ameche hits again at left side for 1 and picks up first down.
1-10-G10 – Moore around left side for 8 (Patton).
2-02-G02 – Ameche plunges over right side for 2 and TD.

Time 12:34. Myhra converts.
Colts 7   Giants 3

Rechichar kicks off short to Rosey Brown, who hands back to Triplett on the 12, returns to 33.

Giants
1-10-G33 – Triplett gains 1 over left tackle.
2-09-G34 – Conerly passes to Rote for 14.
1-10-G48 – Conerly loses 9 attempting to pass.

2-19-G39 – Webster, on double reverse from Gifford, gains 4.

3-15-G43 – Conerly's pass for Gifford is incomplete.

4-15-G43 – Chandler punts to Simpson, who fumbles. Recovered by Guy on the Colts 10.

1-10-C10 – Gifford fumbles on right end sweep and Joyce recovers for Colts on 14.

Colts

1-10-C14 – Unitas's pass to Dupre is incomplete.

2-10-C14 – Unitas hits Berry on sideline for 5.

3-05-C19 – Unitas passes to Ameche on flare for 10.

1-10-C29 – Moore around left side gains 10.

2-10-C39 – Ameche powers over left side for 6.

2-04-C45 – Moore gains 4 on right end sweep.

1-10-C49 – Ameche gains 2 over the center for first down.

1-10-G49 – Unitas hits Berry for 9 but he's out-of-bounds on the catch.

2-10-G49 – Dupre on left end run gains 3.

3-07-G46 – Unitas back to pass scrambles for 16.

1-10-G30 – Moore over right tackle gains 1.

2-09-G29 – Unitas on pass attempt runs for 4 but Colts in-motion.

2-14-G34 – Unitas hits Berry on look-in for 13.

3-01-G21 – Ameche powers right side for 6 and first down.

1-10-G15 – Unitas hits Berry in end zone between Patton and Tunnell for TD.

Time: 1:20. Myhra converts.
Colts 14   Giants 3

Rechichar kicks off into end zone.

Giants

1-10-G20 – King loses 1 on right side.

2-11-G19 – Conerly back to pass is rushed and loses 8.

3-19-G11 – Webster hits left tackle for 9 as half ends.

THIRD QUARTER

Chandler kicks off to Lyles on goal line, returns 19.

Colts

1-10-C19 – Moore gains 5 over left side.

2-05-C24 – Unitas passes to Mutscheller for 8.

1-10-C32 – Moore on a reverse is hit for loss of 7 (Svare).

2-17-C25 – Unitas passes to Berry for 15 on the sideline as Huff runs him out of bounds. Huff clashes with Ewbank on sideline and Shinnick enters into dispute.

3-02-C40 – Dupre carries for 3 but Colts offside.

3-07-C35 – Unitas passes to Dupre for gain of 3.

4-04-C38 – Brown punts to Maynard on 12, returns 9.

Giants

1-10-G21 – Gifford stopped at right side for no gain.

2-10-G21 – Conerly hits Gifford in the flat but loses 3.

3-13-G18 – Conerly buried attempting pass on the 13.

4-18-G13 – Chandler punts to Moore on Colts 41. Fair catch.

Colts

1-10-C41 – Unitas passes to Mutscheller for 32.

1-10-G27 – Dupre over left side gains 1.

2-09-G26 – Unitas passes incomplete for Berry.

3-09-G26 – Unitas hits Berry on left sideline for 11.

1-10-G15 – Unitas flips out to Moore flat for 12.

1-GL-G3 – Ameche hits left side for 2.

2-GTG-G1 – Unitas on sneak is held for no gain.

3-GTG-G1 – Ameche powers into center but stopped for no gain.

4-GTG-G1 – Ameche swings wide to right on pitchout but Livingston tackles him on the 5.

Giants

1-10-G5 – Gifford around left end gains 5.

2-05-G10 – Webster hits over right tackle for 3.

3-02-G13 – Conerly finds Rote behind Colts secondary on a pass and he runs to the Colts 25, where Nelson tackles him from behind. Rote fumbles but the ball picked up on the run by Webster, who is finally knocked out-of-bounds on the Colts 1 by Taseff.

1-GTG-C1 – Webster hits left tackle but stopped.

2-GTG-C1 – Triplett plunges over right guard for TD.

Time: 3:46. Summerall converts.
Colts 14   Giants 10

Chandler kicks off to Simpson on the 2, returns 23.

Colts

1-10-C25 – Dupre gains 2 over right tackle.

2-08-C27 – Unitas caught by Modzelewski attempting to pass for loss of 7.

3-15-C20 – Unitas, attempting to pass, runs for 9.

4-06-C29 – Brown punts to Maynard on Giants 15, returns 4.

Giants

1-10-G19 – Webster plunges over left side for 3.

2-07-G22 – Conerly passes to Schnelker for 17.

1-10-G39 – Quarter ends.

FOURTH QUARTER

1-10-G39 – Conerly hits Schnelker for 46 yards.
1-10-C15 – Conerly passes to Gifford on right sideline and he goes in from the 5 after the catch.

Time: 14:07. Summerall converts.
Giants 17   Colts 14

Chandler kicks off to Simpson in the end zone.

Colts
1-10-C20 – Unitas passes to Moore for 11.
1-10-C31 – Unitas passes to Berry on sideline for 13.
1-10-C44 – Unitas's pass for Dupre is incomplete.
2-10-C44 – Unitas run out of the pocket for 1 (Youso).
3-09-C45 – Unitas's pass for Mutscheller ruled complete as interference on Crow is called at Giants 38.
1-10-G38 – Ameche is stopped for loss of 1.
2-11-G39 – Unitas goes long for Dupre but misses.
3-11-G39 – Unitas's pass for Moore broken up by Huff.
4-11-G39 – Rechichar's FG attempt is short into the end zone from the Giants 46.

Giants
1-10-G20 – King picks up 4 over right tackle.
2-06-G24 – Conerly passes to MacAfee for 15.
1-10-G39 – Gifford loses 2 and offside against Giants is refused.
2-09-G37 – Triplett gains 7 around left end.
3-05-G44 – Gifford on a sweep gains 10 to Colts' 46.
1-10-C46 – Gifford gains 4 on right side.
2-06-C42 – King fumbles handoff and Krouse recovers on Giants 42.

Colts

1-10-G42 – Unitas goes long for Moore at the goal line but reception is ruled as caught out of bounds.

2-10-G42 – Unitas's pass for Berry knocked down by Karilivacz.

3-10-G42 – Unitas hits Berry on left side for 11.

1-10-G31 – Dupre over left side for 4.

2-06-G27 – Unitas hit by Robustelli for loss of 11 on pass.

3-17-G38 – Unitas again hit attempting to pass by Modzelewski for loss of 9.

4-26-G47 – Brown punts to Patton on 5, returns 14.

Giants

1-10-G19 – Webster hits for 5 at right tackle.

2-05-G24 – Gifford on a sweep stopped for no gain.

3-05-G24 – Conerly passes to Webster for 10.

1-10-G34 – Webster gains 1 at left guard.

2-09-G35 – Gifford gains 5 on right side sweep.

3-04-G40 – Gifford on cut back gains 3. Short of first down.

4-01-G43 – Chandler punts to Taseff, fair catch on own 14.

Colts

1-10-C14 – Unitas's pass for Mutscheller is incomplete.

2-10-C14 – Unitas's pass for Dupre is incomplete.

3-10-C14 – Unitas hits Moore over center for 11.

1-10-C25 – Unitas misses Dupre on long pass.

2-10-C25 – Unitas passes to Berry, who runs for 25.

1-10-C50 – Unitas passes to Berry on left sideline for 15.

1-10-G35 – Unitas passes to Berry on left sideline for 22.

1-10-G13 – Myhra kicks 19 yard FG with 7 seconds left.

Colts 17   Giants 17

Rechichar kicks off to Maynard in end zone, returns 18.

Giants

1-10-G18 – Conerly sneaks for no gain. Regulation game ends.

OVERTIME PERIOD

Rote and Svoboda win toss for Giants, who elect to receive. Rechichar kicks off to Maynard on 10, fumbles but recovers and carries to the 20.

Giants

1-10-G20 – Gifford gains 4 over left side.

2-06-G24 – Conerly misses Schnelker with pass.

3-06-G24 – Conerly on a keeper gains 5. Short of first down.

4-01-G29 – Chandler punts to Taseff on 19, returns 1.

Colts

1-10-C20 – Dupre gains 11 on left side cutback.

1-10-C31 – Unitas's long pass for Moore incomplete (Crow).

2-10-C31 – Dupre gains 2 over left tackle.

3-08-C33 – Unitas hits Ameche over middle for 8.

1-10-C41 – Dupre gains 4 at right tackle.

2-06-C45 – Unitas hit by Modzelewski attempting to pass for loss of 8.

3-14-C37 – Unitas hits Berry deep on left sideline for 21.

1-10-G42 – Ameche, on a trap, gains 22 up the middle.

1-10-G20 – Dupre held for no gain.

2-10-G20 – Unitas's pass in left flat for Berry gains 12.

1-GTG-G8 – Ameche gains 1 in center of the line.

2-GTG-G7 – Unitas passes to Mutscheller on right sideline for 6 and out of bounds.

3-GTG-G1 – Ameche plunges over right tackle for TD.

Time 6:45 to play.

Colts 23   Giants 17

TEAM STATISTICS

Colts		Giants
9	First downs rushing	3
17	First downs passing	7
1	First down penalty	0
27	Total first downs	10
138	Yards gained rushing (net)	88
322	Yards gained passing (net)	178
460	Total yards gained	266
27	Yards lost attempting pass	22
40	Passes attempted	18
26	Passes completed	12
0	Intercepted by	1
0	Yards returned by	5
4	Number of punts	6
51	Average distance	48
5	Punts returned by	4
10	Yards punts returned	14
3	Kick-off returned	3
62	Yards kick-offs returned	52
4	Penalties	1
32	Yards penalized	5
2	Fumbles	6
2	Ball lost fumbles	4

Colts.... 0 14 0 3 6 — 23
Giants.... 3 0 7 7 0 — 17

Giants—Touchdowns, Triplett (1-yard run); Gifford (15-yard pass from Conerly). Extra points-Summerall 2 (placements). Field goal-Summerall (36 yards).

Colts—Touchdowns, Ameche 2 (2-yard run; 1-yard run). Berry (15-yard pass from Unitas). Extra point-Myhra 2 (placements). Field goal-Myhra (19 yards).

CHAMPIONSHIP GAME RECORDS

The Colts and Giants set a dozen records for NFL champion-ship game competition:

- Raymond Berry, Colts end, caught 12 passes for 178 yards. He bettered the previous high of 11 passes set by Dante Lavelli of the Browns in the 1950 title game with the Rams.
- Berry's yardage broke the previous high of 160 yards gained by Wane Millner of the Redskins against the Bears during the 1937 title game.
- John Unitas, Colts quarterback, set a record of 349 yards gained on passes in a championship game. He broke the old mark of 335 set by Sammy Baugh of the Redskins against the Bears in the 1937 title game.
- The Colts set a record of 17 first downs on passes, breaking the mark of 16 set by the Browns in the 1951 title game against the Rams. The Colts' total of 27 first downs broke the old record of 22 set by the Eagles against the Cardinals in 1947 and has been tied in six games since then.

Most fumbles in championship game – Giants, 6.

Most opponent fumbles recovered in one game – Colts, 4.

FINANCIAL STATEMENT

Paid attendance – 64,185

Gross receipts, including radio-TV – $698,646

Taxes and rental – $129,894

Game operating expenses – $36,879

Net receipts – $531,872

Player pool (70 percent of net) – $372,310

Each winning share – $4,718 (42 ½ shares)

Each losing share – $3,111 (42 ½ shares)

Pool for divisional second-place clubs – $37,231

INDIVIDUAL STATISTICS

COLTS
Rushing

	Attempts	Yards
Alan Ameche	14	65
Lenny Moore	8	23
L. G. Dupre	11	30
John Unitas	6	20

GIANTS
Rushing

	Attempts	Yards
Frank Gifford	12	60
Alex Webster	12	24
Mel Triplett	5	12
Charlie Conerly	2	5
Phil King	3	-13

Passing (Colts)

	Att.	Comp.	Yards
John Unitas	40	26	349

Passing (Giants)

	Att.	Comp.	Yards
Charlie Conerly	14	10	187
Don Heinrich	4	2	13

Receiving (Colts)

	No.	Yards
Raymond Berry	12	178
Lenny Moore	6	101
Jim Mutscheller	3	46
Alan Ameche	3	17
L. G. Dupre	2	7

Receiving (Giants)

	No.	Yards
Bob Schnelker	2	76
Kyle Rote	2	63
Alex Webster	2	16
Frank Gifford	3	15
Mel Triplett	2	15
Ken MacAfee	1	15

Note: Total yardage gained credited to individual passers and receivers but losses deducted from team passing total according to NFL rules.

INDIVIDUAL LEADERS FOR ENTIRE SEASON

PASSING
Colts

	Att.	Comp.	Int.	Yds.	L.G.	Tds.	Pct.
John Unitas	263	136	7	2007	77	19	.517
George Shaw	89	41	4	531	57	7	.461
Ray Brown	2	1	0	-1	-1	0	.500

Giants

	Att.	Comp.	Int.	Yds.	L.G.	Tds.	Pct.
Charlie Conerly	184	88	9	1199	44	10	.478
Don Heinrich	68	26	2	369	41	4	.382
Frank Gifford	10	3	1	109	63	1	.300

SCORING
Colts

	TD	EP	FG	Pts.
Lenny Moore	14	0	0	84
Steve Myhra	0	48	4	60
Alan Ameche	9	0	0	54
Raymond Berry	9	0	0	54
Jim Mutscheller	7	0	0	42
Lenny Lyles	4	0	0	24
L.G. Dupre	3	0	0	18
John Unitas	3	0	0	18
Bert Rechichar	1	0	1	9
Andy Nelson	1	0	0	6
Billy Pricer	1	0	0	6
George Shaw	1	0	0	6

Giants

	TD	EP	FG	Pts.
Pat Summerall	0	28	12	64
Frank Gifford	10	0	0	60
Alex Webster	6	0	0	36
Bob Schnelker	5	0	0	30
Kyle Rote	3	0	0	18
Ken MacAfee	2	0	0	12
Phil King	1	0	0	6
Mel Triplett	1	0	0	6
Don Heinrich	1	0	0	6
Carl Karilivacz	1	0	0	6

RECEIVING
Colts

	No.	Yds.	L.G.	TDs
Raymond Berry	56	794	54	9
Lenny Moore	51	943	77	7
Jim Mutscheller	27	499	54	7
L.G. Dupre	13	111	22	0
Alan Ameche	13	81	18	1
Lenny Lyles	5	24	11	1
Jack Call	4	28	12	0
Bert Rechichar	3	23	12	1
Billy Pricer	3	14	6	0
Art DeCarlo	1	10	10	0
Bill Pellington	1	-1	-1	0

Giants

	No.	Yds.	L.G.	TDs
Frank Gifford	29	330	41	2
Alex Webster	25	279	37	3
Bob Schnelker	24	460	63	5
Kyle Rote	12	244	44	3
Phil King	11	132	35	0
Mel Triplett	7	110	32	0
Don Maynard	5	84	31	0
Ken MacAfee	5	52	22	2
Bob Mischak	1	27	27	0

RUSHING
Colts

	Att.	Yds.	L.G.	Avg.
Alan Ameche	171	791	28	4.6
Lenny Moore	82	598	7	7.3
L.G. Dupre	95	390	39	4.2
John Call	37	154	35	4.1
John Unitas	33	139	28	4.2
Lenny Lyles	22	41	27	1.9
Billy Pricer	10	26	4	2.6
George Shaw	5	-3	3	-0.6
Bay Brown	1	-9	-9	-9.0

Giants

	Att.	Yds.	L.G.	Avg.
Frank Gifford	115	468	33	4.1
Mel Triplett	118	466	24	3.9
Alex Webster	110	398	54	4.0
Phil King	73	316	38	4.2
Don Maynard	12	45	14	3.8
Billy Lott	4	30	12	7.5
Don Chandler	1	15	15	15.0

PUNTING
Colts

	No.	Avg.	Lg.
Raymond Brown	41	39.9	60
Dick Horn	19	34.0	48
Avatus Stone	1	28.0	28
L. G. Dupre	1	-4.0	-4

Giants

	No.	Avg.	Lg.
Don Chandler	65	44.0	67

PUNT RETURNS
Colts

	No.	Yds.	L.G.	Avg.
Carl Taseff	29	196	33	6.9
Bert Rechichar	7	29	11	4.1
Lenny Moore	2	11	11	5.1
Jackie Simpson	1	1	1	1.0

Giants

	No.	Yds.	L.G.	Avg.
Don Heinrich	5	-4	6	0.0
Don Maynard	24	117	22	4.9
Charlie Conerly	12	-17	11	0.0
Lindon Crow	11	46	34	4.2
Jim Patton	1	5	5	5.0
Emlen Tunnell	6	0	0	0.0

INTERCEPTIONS
Colts

	Att.	Yds.	L.G.	Avg.
Andy Nelson	8	199	69	24.9
Raymond Brown	8	149	30	18.6
Carl Taseff	7	52	17	7.4
Bill Pellington	4	44	21	11.0
Milt Davis	4	40	28	10.0
Don Shinnick	3	23	16	7.7
Leo Sanford	1	7	7	7.0

Giants

	Att.	Yds.	L.G.	Avg.
Jim Patton	11	183	42	16.6
Lindon Crow	3	40	43	13.3
Carl Karilivacz	3	15	15	5.0
Sam Huff	2	23	15	11.5
Harland Svare	1	25	25	25.0
Emlen Tunnell	1	8	8	8.0

KICK-OFF RETURNS
Colts

	No.	Yds.	L.G.	Avg.
Leonard Lyles	11	398	103	36.2
Billy Pricer	9	168	28	18.7
Lenny Moore	4	91	25	22.8
Jackie Simpson	3	59	24	19.7
Bert Rechichar	3	50	22	16.7
Jack Call	2	48	26	24.0
Carl Taseff	1	50	50	50.0
Art DeCarlo	1	0	0	0.0

Giants

	No.	Yds.	L.G.	Avg.
Don Maynard	11	284	44	25.8
Phil King	13	279	31	21.5
Billy Lott	5	78	24	15.6
Mel Triplett	4	59	20	14.8
Roosevelt Brown	1	0	0	0.0

SEASON STATISTICS

Colts	Opp.	Category	Giants	Opp.
253	188	First downs	183	170
4539	3284	Total yards gained	3330	3418
2127	1291	Yards rushing	1725	1440
2412	1993	Yards passing	1605	1978
456	331	No. rushes	450	400
354	363	No. passes	266	311
178	168	Passes completed	119	142
50.3	46.3	Completion %	44.7	45.7
35	11	Interceptions by	21	12
36.7	44.1	Punting average	44.0	41.7
6.1	4.4	Punt return average	4.0	7.3
25.4	28.8	Kickoff-return average	20.5	22.2
534	555	Yards penalized	379	451
26	26	Fumbles	29	35
17	11	Opp. fumbles recovered	19	14

COLTS			GIANTS		
** Won 9, lost 3			***Won 9, lost 3**		
28	Detroit	15	37	Cards (Buffalo)	7
51	Chicago Bears	38	24	Philadelphia (a)	27
24	Green Bay (Milwaukee)	17	21	Washington (a)	14
40	Detroit (a)	14	6	Chicago Cards	23
35	Washington	10	17	Pittsburgh	6
56	Green Bay	0	21	Cleveland (a)	17
21	New York (a)	24	24	Baltimore	21
17	Chicago Bears (a)	0	10	Pittsburgh (a)	31
34	Los Angeles	7	30	Washington	0
35	San Francisco	27	24	Philadelphia	10
28	Los Angeles (a)	30	19	Detroit (a)	17
12	San Francisco	21	13	Cleveland	10
381		203	246		183

**Defeated New York in championship, 23-17.   *Defeated Cleveland in playoff, 10-0.

COLTS ROSTER

No.	Player	Pos.	Wt.	Ht.	Age	College	Yrs. Pro
14	Shaw, George	QB	190	6-0	25	Oregon	4
17	Brown, Raymond	QB-HB	195	6-2	22	Mississippi	1
19	Unitas, John	QB	190	6-1	25	Louisville	3
20	Davis, Milt	HB	190	6-1	29	U.C.L.A.	2
21	DeCarlo, Art	HB	196	6-2	27	Georgia	4
23	Taseff, Carl	HB	190	5-11	30	John Carroll	7
24	Moore, Lenny	HB	190	6-1	25	Penn State	3
25	Call, John	HB	200	6-1	23	Colgate	2
26	Lyles, Leonard	HB	198	6-2	22	Louisville	1
31	Pricer, Billy	FB	210	5-10	23	Oklahoma	2
35	Ameche, Alan	FB	220	6-1	25	Wisconsin	4
36	Pellington, Bill	LB	230	6-2	31	Rutgers	6
41	Simpson, Jackie	HB	180	5-10	24	Florida	1
44	Rechichar, Bert	HB	210	6-1	28	Tennessee	7
45	Dupre, L.G.	HB	190	5-11	26	Baylor	4
47	Sample, John	HB	203	6-1	21	Maryland State	1
50	Nutter, Madison	C	235	6-4	27	Va. Polytechnic	5
52	Szymanski, Dick	C-LB	230	6-1	25	Notre Dame	3
55	Sanford, Leo	LB	230	6-1	29	Louisiana Tech	8
60	Preas, George	T	245	6-2	25	Va. Polytechnic	4
63	Spinney, Art	G	230	6-1	31	Boston College	7
64	Thurston, Fred	G	245	6-1	25	Valparaiso	1
65	Myhra, Steve	G	235	6-1	24	North Dakota	2
66	Shinnick, Don	LB	230	6-0	23	U.C.L.A.	2
68	Sandusky, Alex	G	235	6-3	26	Clarion	5
70	Donovan, Art	T	270	6-3	33	Boston College	9
76	Lipscomb, Gene	T	288	6-6	27	Miller (Det.) High	6
77	Parker, Jim	T	270	6-3	24	Ohio State	2
78	Krouse, Ray	T	278	6-3	31	Maryland	8
79	Plunkett, Sherman	T	265	6-4	25	Maryland State	1
80	Nelson, Andy	HB	180	6-1	25	Memphis State	2
81	Braase, Ordell	E	215	6-4	26	South Dakota	2
82	Berry, Raymond	E	190	6-2	25	S. M. U.	4
83	Joyce, Don	E	255	6-3	29	Tulane	8
84	Mutscheller, Jim	E	215	6-1	28	Notre Dame	5
89	Marchetti, Gino	E	240	6-4	31	San Francisco	7

GIANTS ROSTER

No.	Player	Pos.	Wt.	Ht.	Age	College	Yrs. Pro
11	Heinrich, Don	QB	180	6-0	27	Washington	5
13	Maynard, Don	HB	178	6-0	22	Texas Western	1
16	Gifford, Frank	HB	205	6-1	28	S. California	7
17	Kemp, Jack	QB	200	6-2	24	Occidental	2
20	Patton, Jim	HB	180	5-10	26	Mississippi	4
21	Karilivacz, Carl	HB	190	6-1	27	Syracuse	6
22	Lott, Billy	HB	195	6-0	23	Mississippi	1
24	King, Phil	FB	225	6-4	22	Vanderbilt	1
29	Webster, Alex	HB	210	6-3	27	N. C. State	4
30	Svoboda, Bill	LB	215	6-0	29	Tulane	9
33	Triplett, Mel	FB	215	6-1	26	Toledo	4
34	Chandler, Don	HB	205	6-2	23	Florida	3
41	Crow, Lindon	HB	200	6-1	25	S. California	4
42	Conerly, Charlie	QB	185	6-1	37	Mississippi	11
44	Rote, Kyle	E	205	6-0	30	S.M.U.	8
45	Tunnell, Emlen	HB	200	6-1	33	Iowa	11
48	Hughes, Ed	HB	180	6-1	28	Tulsa	4
55	Wietecha, Ray	C	225	6-1	29	Northwestern	6
60	Guy, Melwood	G-T	248	6-3	23	Duke	1
62	Mischak, Bob	G	230	6-0	25	Army	1
66	Stroud, Jack	G	235	6-1	29	Tennessee	6
68	Barry, Al	G	230	6-2	26	S. California	3
70	Huff, Sam	LB	230	6-1	23	West Virginia	3
71	Brackett, M.L.	T	250	6-5	25	Auburn	3
72	Youso, Frank	T	260	6-4	22	Minnesota	1
75	Katcavage, Jim	T	230	6-3	23	Dayton	3
76	Grier, Roosevelt	T	270	6-5	25	Penn State	3
77	Modzelewski, Dick	T	260	6-0	27	Maryland	6
79	Brown, Roosevelt	T	245	6-3	25	Morgan State	6
80	MacAfee, Ken	E	215	6-2	29	Alabama	5
81	Robustelli, Andy	E	230	6-1	30	Arnold	8
84	Svare, Harland	LB	215	6-0	27	Wash. State	6
85	Schnelker, Bob	E	215	6-4	28	Bowling Green	6
88	Summerall, Pat	E	235	6-4	28	Arkansas	7
89	Livingston, Cliff	LB	215	6-3	28	UCLA	5

INDEX

ABOUT THE AUTHOR

Lou Sahadi is one of the country's most prolific sports authors. He has collaborated on the official autobiographies of Len Dawson, Don Shula, Willie Mays, Hank Stram, and the consummate biography of Johnny Unitas. His first book, *The Long Pass,* was selected for the Nixon Presidential Library. *One Sunday in December* is his twenty-first book. He lives in Boca Raton, Florida.